R A I L S
A C R O S S T H E
TUNDRA

A HISTORICAL ALBUM OF THE ALASKA RAILROAD

R A I L S
ACROSS THE
TUNDRA

A HISTORICAL ALBUM OF THE ALASKA RAILROAD

By
Stan Cohen

PICTORIAL HISTORIES PUBLISHING COMPANY
MISSOULA, MONTANA

LIBRARY OF CONGRESS
CONTROL NUMBER 84-60465

ISBN 0-933126-43-3

First Printing: July 1984
Second Printing: May 1986
Third Printing: April 1988
Fourth Printing: April 1992
Fifth Printing: March 1995
Sixth Printing: March 1998
Seventh Printing: March 2001

Typography: Arrow Graphics, Missoula, Montana
Cover Art Work: Allen Woodard, Missoula, Montana

PHOTO SOURCES
AHFAM: Anchorage Historical and Fine Arts Museum
AHL: Alaska Historical Library, Juneau
UAA: University of Alaska Archives, Fairbanks
UW: University of Washington Special Collections, Seattle
USA: U.S. Army Archives, Washington, D.C.

PRINTED IN CANADA BY FRIESENS, ALTONA, MANITOBA

PICTORIAL HISTORIES PUBLISHING CO., INC.
713 South Third St. W., Missoula, Montana 59801
Phone (406) 549-8488 FAX (406) 728-9280
E-Mail—phpc@montana.com
Website—pictorialhistoriespublishing.com

TABLE OF CONTENTS

INTRODUCTION

Like the transcontinental railroads of the American West, the Alaska Railroad opened up vast new frontiers for settlement. It was completed in 1923 and spawned cities along its route. It is, and probably will remain, the last of the major rail lines to be hacked out of the North American wilderness.

Now entering its seventh decade of operation, the railroad is still a vital part of Alaska's economy. Not only does it haul thousands of tons of goods between the coast and the interior, it also takes tourists and other travelers through some of the most beautiful scenery in the world.

Unlike most of the nation's railroads, the Alaska Railroad was totally financed and constructed by the United States government. Construction began at about the time of the completion of the Panama Canal, one of the largest construction projects the world has ever known. Although they were separated by thousands of miles, the railroad and the canal shared some of the same supervisory personnel and equipment, and both opened up major commercial arteries.

One can also draw an analogy between the construction of the railroad and the building of the Alaskan oil pipeline in the mid-20th century. Both were built at great cost and difficulty and both were built to transport goods through the wilds of America's last frontier.

There is no doubt that the 470-mile railroad has done as much for Alaska as any other single project in the state's history. For instance, Alaska's major city, Anchorage, came into being as a result of the railroad. Fairbanks, which had started out early in the century as a booming gold-rush town, became a focal point of all of Alaska's interior. Seward, at the railroad's southern terminus, took on tremendous importance at the onset of construction.

As the state enters its second quarter-century, the railroad is assuming an increasingly important role in Alaska's economy. Both freight and passenger traffic are on the upswing, and the railroad, which is about to change ownership, is playing a vital part in the development of the state's natural resources.

Thousands of fine historical photographs exist of the railroad's construction and development. I have tried to portray the line's history by selecting several hundred photos that best tell the story. This book also includes a short narrative to provide background information for the photographs.

For the complete photographic history of the railroad, one should consult Bernadine L. Prince's monumental two-volume work, *The Alaska Railroad in Pictures, 1914-1964,* which has been out of print for years but is available in many libraries. Several very good narratives of the railroad have been published in recent years, including Edwin M. Fitch's *The Alaska Railroad* and William H. Wilson's *Railroad in the Clouds: The Alaska Railroad in the Age of Steam, 1914-1945.*

The main depositories for Alaska Railroad photographs are in the National Archives, Washington, D.C., and at the archives of the Anchorage Historical and Fine Arts Museum. I am deeply indebted to Mrs. M. Diane Brenner, photo archivist at the Anchorage Museum, for her help in obtaining photographs and information over a two-year period. I also wish to thank the staffs of the Alaska State Library in Juneau and the University of Alaska Archives in Fairbanks for their kind help. Other photographs were obtained from the U.S. Army and from private sources.

The Alaska Railroad itself was very helpful with general information, with statistics and in providing trips to points along the route. A special thanks to railroad personnel John Killoran and James Blasingame for their encouragement, suggestions and review of my manuscript.

Finally, I hope this album will in a small way help to preserve the history of one of the outstanding attractions of the Great Land. I urge anyone who is planning a journey North to consider taking a trip on this fascinating railroad.

Stan Cohen
June 1984

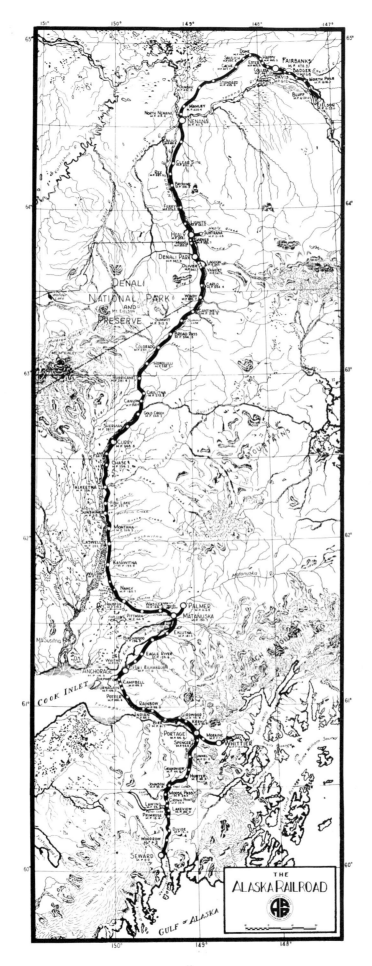

THE
ALASKA RAILROAD

Driving the first spike on the "Government Railroad" at Ship Creek, April 20, 1915.

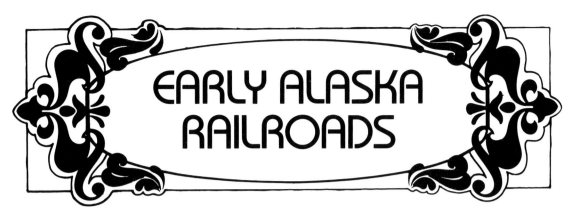

EARLY ALASKA RAILROADS

S everal other railroads in Alaska were constructed prior to the Alaska Railroad, one of which was the predecessor to the ARR. The earliest was the White Pass and Yukon Route, which had its southern terminus at Skagway and was intended to provide a route from tidewater, over the mountains of the Coast Range, to White-horse and the Yukon goldfields.

Construction of the narrow-gauge line began in 1898 and proceeded over the White Pass to the Yukon River at Whitehorse, Yukon. This railroad, with 20 miles of its 110-mile length located in Alaska, was finished in 1900. It remained in operation until 1982 when the mines in the Yukon were shut down due to economic conditions.

The other major railroad in Alaska was the Copper River and Northwestern Railroad, built between 1906 and 1911 from Cordova, on Prince William Sound, north for 195 miles to a huge copper ore deposit in the Wrangell Mountains. Both this and the White Pass were constructed under the supervision of the well-known railroad builder Michael J. Heney.

The copper deposit was owned by the Alaska Syndicate, controlled by J.P. Morgan and the Guggenheim family. The syndicate eventually bought the CR and NW. In the late 1930s, the copper deposit was worked out and the railroad was officially abandoned in 1939.

Alaska Central/Alaska Northern Railroad

One railroad, the Alaska Central, figured prominently in the history of the Alaska Railroad. Though it was never completed, its intended route was almost the same as that used later by the ARR. It also was one of the prime reasons that prompted the U.S. government to take part in the construction of the Alaska Railroad.

The Alaska Central Railroad Co. was incorporated in the state of Washington in 1902 by a group of Seattle businessmen. Its purpose was to provide a route that was completely in U.S. territory and that would lead toward the Yukon River system and, thus, the Klondike, Fairbanks and Nome goldfields. The route was to go from Seward, on Resurrection Bay, through the Susitna Valley and over Broad Pass to a terminus on the Tanana River. From there, passengers could board river boats to Dawson and the goldfields.

The intended route was virtually the same as that used later by the Alaska Railroad. When gold was discovered on the banks of the Chena River in 1903, the Alaska Central's planners decided they would push their route even farther north to the then-bustling gold rush town of Fairbanks.

Construction was started north from Seward, then a new town, on Aug. 23, 1904. By the end of the year, 20 miles of track had been completed and the railroad was in operation. The immediate

Surveying party at Kern Creek, Alaska Central, 1905. AHFAM

objective was to reach the rich Matanuska Valley coalfields as soon as possible.

Over the next few years, the railroad acquired new financing and rolling stock and by 1910 it had completed 51 miles of track. It was during this time that construction of the famous loop trestle, used by successive railroads until 1951, was started near Mile 49.

In the aftermath of the Panic of 1907, the railroad was forced into receivership in 1908, and was re-organized as the Alaska Northern Railway Co. The new company, chartered in the state of Washington and backed by Canadian money and Seattle businessmen, assumed ownership of three of the Alaska Central's locomotives as well as freight and baggage cars, other rolling stock, and the 51 miles of track.

Construction resumed and an additional 21 miles of track was completed. The loop was finished and trains now ran as far as Kern Creek on Turnagain Arm, where the trains could transfer their freight to boats that could haul it to the junction with the Iditarod Trail.

Plans were made to continue construction to Fairbanks along the surveyed route of the former Alaska Central, but funds ran out and construction was halted. This was typical of many of the nation's railroads, but railroads in Alaska faced unusually severe problems due to high freight costs, the difficulty of constructing roadbed, and the small market potential.

Without money to continue construction, or even to operate, the railroad faced additional problems—its equipment and roadbed began to deteriorate. The 72 miles of rail was purchased by the U.S. government in 1915 for 25 cents on the dollar.

The Alaska Central's first spike is set at the Seward dock on April 16, 1904. The railroad was to put down 51 miles of track north from Seward before going into receivership in 1908. AHFAM (Alaska RR Collection)

Construction trains on the Alaska Central Railroad. Top: 1904. Bottom: 1905. UW Special Collections

CONSTRUCTION TRAIN.
ALASKA CENTRAL R. R. JUNE 1905.
EVANS PHOTO.

Engine #1, the first engine of the new Alaska Central Railroad, arrived at Seward in 1904. A 4-4-0 built in 1883 for the Northern Pacific, it was later used by the Alaska Northern and by the Alaska Railroad.
AHFAM (Alaska RR Collection)

Construction train crossing a long trestle near Seward, August 1905. UW Special Collections

Construction train at Mile 48, Alaska Central Railroad, August 1906.
AHFAM (Alaska RR Collection)

Fourth of July excursion party at Mile 46 on the Alaska Central Railroad, 1906.
AHFAM (Alaska RR Collection)

Bucking a snowslide at Mile 44 of the Alaska Central. This slide is still a major problem today.
AHFAM (Alaska RR Collection)

Gasoline-powered car #2 at Mile 52 of the Alaska Northern. This car was used to haul passengers when traffic was too light for the regularly-scheduled steam trains.
AHFAM (Alaska RR Collection)

Line reconstruction, Mile 41, Alaska Northern. The Alaska Central/Northern had very poor roadbed construction, thus the entire line was in very poor condition when the Alaska Engineering Commission took it over. AHFAM (Alaska RR Collection)

Bridge #41.5, Mile 21.5, Alaska Northern.
AHFAM (Alaska RR Collection)

Alaska Northern's bridge #47, over Trail Creek at Mile 33.
AHFAM (Alaska RR Collection)

1911 (?)

TIME ..TABLE..

ALASKA NORTHERN RAILWAY

SEWARD, ALASKA

COMPLIMENTS
Methodist :: Episcopal :: Church

North Bound				South Bound
No. 1	Distance			No. 2
Daily Except Sunday	From Seward	STATIONS		Daily Except Sunday
A. M.				P. M.
7 30		Seward		5 00
7 50	6 5	Bear Creek		4 45
8 15	12 0	Summit		4 20
*8 40	18 0	Lake Kenai		*3 55
9 00	23 5	Roosevelt		3 40
*9 08	26 0	Falls Creek		*3 37
9 15	29 5	Moose Pass Junction		3 25
9 30	34 0	Sunrise Junction		3 10
9 45	40 5	Hunters		2 55
10 25	52 0	Tunnel Siding		2 15
10 30	53 0	Spencer Glacier		2 10
11 15	65 0	Twenty Mile River		1 25
11 40		End of Track		1 00

*Flag Stations—Stop only on signal for passengers.

A 1911 Alaska Northern Railway timetable.

Tanana Valley Railroad

This little railroad was the only visible evidence of a dream to link by rail many towns in Alaska's interior and in the Yukon during the early 20th century. The railroad operated for a time, but eventually it was purchased by the U.S. government, which intended to use some of its assets for the Alaska Railroad.

The Tanana Valley Railroad was incorporated in 1904 by Falcon Joslin, a Fairbanks attorney and former businessman, and it was backed by financial interests in New York and Chicago. The railroad's original plans were to link Fairbanks with Circle City, Nome, Haines, and Dawson, in the Yukon.

The Tanana Valley Railroad, however, never reached more than 44.7 miles in length. A three-foot, narrow-gauge, single-track was laid to Chena and later to Nenana. From Chena the line ran nine miles to Fairbanks, another branch extended 35 miles from Fairbanks northeast to Chatanika gold-mining district. In 1923 the narrow-gauge was changed to the standard-gauge along its entire length.

Fairbanks often had been cut off from access to the Tanana River due to low water in the Chena River, and the railroad was supposed to alleviate the problem. But the roadbed was built partly over low, swampy ground and little ballast was used in its construction. During high water, this part of the roadbed, along with several pile trestle bridges, was sometimes washed away.

Over $867,000 was spent in constructing the railroad. Still, the builders avoided the expense of heavy grading, and they laid the grade line close to the ground. The ridges were climbed by using steep gradients, and the valleys were crossed on wooden trestles.

The railroad began operations in 1905. Rolling stock consisted of four locomotives, 30 freight cars, and four passenger cars. Two of the locomotives were obtained from the White Pass and Yukon Route (a Brooks 2-6-0 and a Baldwin 4-4-0). A Porter 0-4-0 was purchased from the Northern Light, Power, Coal and Transportation Co. and is now on display at Alaskaland in Fairbanks.

For most of its years, the railroad made money. Between 1909 and 1914 an annual average of over 40,000 passengers and 15,000 tons of freight made their way along the line, although starting in 1914 the figures began to decline. By 1917 revenue from passengers and freight was barely enough to meet operating expenses. The problems were due to the cessation of gold mining, scarcity of wood fuel, and the relatively low purchasing power of gold during World War I.

In 1917, when the little narrow-gauge was on the brink of bankruptcy, it was purchased by the U.S. government, which had gotten involved in the construction of the Alaska Railroad. The government wanted the Tanana Valley's right-of-way into Fairbanks as well as the station and terminal facilities the railroad owned in the city.

At the time of acquisition, it was also thought that if the goldfields reopened, the Tanana Valley's route to the mining district would become a valuable feeder to the main line of the Alaska Railroad. This feeder line, planners believed, could also haul low-cost coal from the Nenana coalfields to the goldfields, where it would be used to fuel gold-mining operations.

Engine #2, a 4-4-0, Class F-1 Baldwin locomotive built in 1881 for the Northern Pacific. This photo was taken at Hunter, Mile 40, Alaska Northern.

AHFAM (Alaska RR Collection)

The Porter 0-4-0 saddle-tanker engine, the first engine of the Tanana Mines Railroad, on the Chatanika run, 1906.   AHFAM (Alaska RR Collection)

A narrow-gauge Baldwin 4-4-0, built in 1878 for the Olympia and Tenino Railway, is shown working at a gravel pit one and one-half miles from Fairbanks, 1917. The engine was acquired by the Tanana Valley Railroad, then by the A.E.C. It was scrapped in 1930.

AHL (Alaska RR Collection)

CONSTRUCTION & OPERATIONS

It was the discovery of gold and the desire for quality coal for use in a proposed coastal copper smelter that set men thinking about a railroad in Alaska. Gold strikes in the Yukon and at Fairbanks and Nome in the late 1890s and early 1900s led to the first efforts to build a railroad from the ice-free ports of southern Alaska to the gold-fields of the interior. The Alaska Railroad was born as a result of these early efforts.

The Alaska Central Railroad, begun in 1903 and privately financed, was the predecessor to the Alaska Railroad. It was to stretch from Seward far into Alaska's interior, but only 70-some miles of track were actually constructed. The Alaska Central and its successor, the Alaska Northern, both failed financially.

After these and other failures, Congress decided to address the matter of rail transportation in the North. On Aug. 2, 1912, Congress passed the Alaska Territorial Act which contained a section directing President William H. Taft to appoint a commission to examine and survey Alaska's transportation network.

The Alaska Railroad Commission, as the body came to be known, took stock of the failures of several railroads in Alaska and scandals in other privately financed railroads elsewhere in the United States. It also took into account the immense size of Alaska, its small population, and its large deposits of minerals. With these factors in mind, the commission determined that the only

The Alaska Engineering Commission in 1919. Left to right: Col. F. Mears, chairman and chief engineer; C.L. Mason, chief clerk; William Gerig, assistant chief engineer; H.P. Warren, chief of supply division; F. Horser, engineer for maintenance and construction; B.H. Barndollar, examiner of accounts and legal advisor. AHL (Alaska RR Collection)

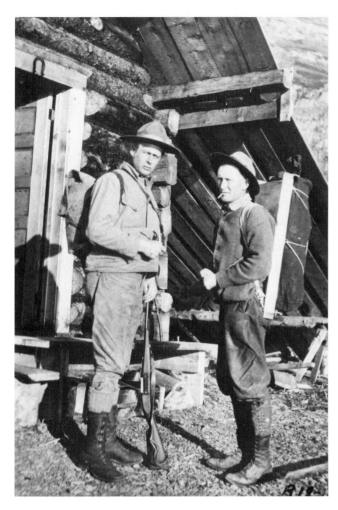

A.E.C. commissioners Frederick Mears, left, and Thomas Riggs, Jr., right, at Ship Creek, 1914.
AHFAM (Alaska RR Collection)

type of railroad with a chance of success in Alaska was one that would be financed—and probably operated—by the government.

After a quick survey during the fall of 1912, the commission issued a report recommending two possible routes that would connect the ice-free ports to Alaska's interior. One route would extend the existing Copper River and Northwestern line from Cordova to Fairbanks; the other would link the Alaska Northern line, which stretched some 70 miles north of Seward, to the Fairbanks mining district. The commission did not make a decision on either route.

Acting on the commission's recommendations, Congress on March 12, 1914, passed legislation enabling Taft's successor, President Woodrow Wilson, to construct and operate railroads in the Territory of Alaska. Yet this legislation placed certain restrictions on the construction of a railroad—the railroad could not be longer than 1,000 miles, it had to connect a port both with interior coal mines and a navigable river in the interior, and it could

not exceed a total cost of $35 million.

Two months later, on May 2, 1914, the Alaska Engineering Commission (A.E.C.) was established by the president, acting through his secretary of the interior. Three commissioners were appointed: Lt. Frederick Mears, an experienced engineer who had been head engineer of the Panama Railroad; Thomas Riggs, Jr., of the Alaska Boundary Survey Commission; and William C. Edes, a renowned railroad engineer with many years experience in the West. Though not a member of the commission, Alaska's delegate to Congress, James Wickersham, was an ardent supporter of the project.

Edes was appointed chairman of the commission, and a headquarters was established in Seward. The A.E.C. looked at both routes proposed by the former Alaska Railroad Commission, but spent most of its time examining the "western" or "Susitna" route. Incorporating the former Alaska Northern line, this route extended from Seward to Fairbanks. Along it were areas that showed great promise for the development of coal mining, gold mining and agriculture.

Commissioner W.C. Edes of the A.E.C.
AHFAM (Alaska RR Collection)

-12-

One of the earliest photos of the Alaska Railroad, showing construction material being unloaded at Ship Creek (the future site of Anchorage) in April 1915.   Lyman Woodman, Anchorage

Car trucks brought up from the Panama Railroad are stockpiled waiting to be converted from the 5' gauge to the standard 4' 8-1/2" gauge.   AHL (Alaska RR Collection)

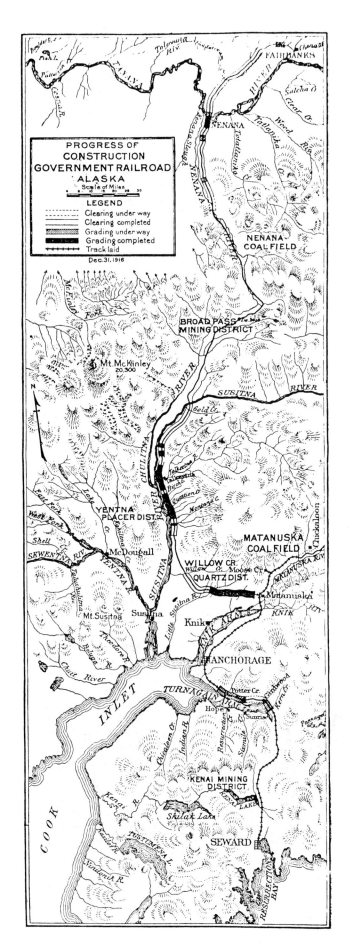

Interior of tunnel #2, October 1919.
AHL (Alaska RR Collection)

On April 10, 1915, after studying the A.E.C.'s report, President Wilson decided on the western route. Word of the recommendation had already leaked out, however, and a mad rush was already underway to Seward, a place that was sure to boom with jobs and business opportunities.

This would not be just another railroad. Hacked out of the wilderness, it would require an enormous structure of supporting services. The commission was authorized to construct and maintain telephone and telegraph lines, build and operate terminal facilities at Seward and along the Tanana River, operate power plants for towns along the route, develop and operate coal mines, establish townsites and sell lots, operate schools and hospitals, and, to keep a steady supply of goods flowing to this huge undertaking, the commission was authorized to open a purchasing office in Seattle.

Preparations began. Riggs took charge of the first detailed location of the line, while Mears was put in charge of construction, which was to begin at the point where Ship Creek enters Knik Arm, the site of present-day Anchorage. The Alaska Northern was purchased for about $16,000 a mile, and it was upgraded to handle the increased loads. Construction materials and men poured into the port of Seward and the Ship Creek area. Finally, in early 1915, construction got underway. It would take eight years and $60 million to finish the project.

South-end portals of tunnels #2 and #3, October 1919.   AHFAM (Alaska RR Collection)

Telegraph wire stockpiled at Seward for use on the railroad telegraph line.
AHL (Alaska RR Collection)

The famous loop section of the railroad, Mile 51.   Author's Collection

Loop at Mile 51, Kenai Peninsula.   UAA (Charles Bunnell Collection)

The "Loop" during World War II, showing switchbacks constructed to bypass the trestles.

The logistics were staggering. The railroad was being constructed through an almost unpopulated wilderness. This meant that construction camps had to be largely self-contained and self-sufficient, that ocean docks, machine shops, and even whole towns had to be built from the ground up, and that rolling stock, construction equipment and various supplies had to be shipped from the West Coast of the United States, some 2,000 miles away.

The West Coast was only one source of supplies for the railroad. The commission sent a representative to Panama who procured machinery and overhauled rolling stock that had been used in the construction of the newly opened Panama Canal.

The commission found a third source of supplies in Alaska's abundant natural resources. Timber reservations were established along the route to provide ties as well as piling and culvert timber, and sawmills were built to supply lumber for the construction of buildings. At first, coal for the locomotives was brought up from Seattle, but in 1916 a small mine was opened at Moose Creek in the Matanuska area. In 1917, an existing mine at Eska Creek was taken over by the railroad, and after that date sufficient coal was mined to fulfill the needs of both the railroad and the towns along its route. As the railroad headed north, other mines eventually were opened in the Chickaloon and Nenana coalfields.

Still, not all the supplies could be found locally, and as construction progressed, transporting supplies from the West Coast to Alaska became an increasingly severe problem, especially after the outbreak of World War I. In part, this was because the railroad was at the mercy of the steamship companies, with their changing schedules and high freight charges. In 1917, however, the A.E.C. began to charter its own ships and barges, as it did to transport equipment north from Panama, and the move resulted in savings of time as well as money.

During the first part of the railroad's construction, the bulk of the supplies from the south were unloaded at Seward, which was the railroad's only deepwater port as well as its construction headquarters. But eventually Anchorage, then a new town on Ship Creek, became an important construction camp. The railroad's permanent headquarters were moved there in 1917, but Seward retained a division headquarters, which had been set up in 1917 to rehabilitate the line of the defunct Alaska Northern.

The men who built the Alaska Railroad were, for the most part, recent European immigrants, just as the men who built the early transcontinental railroads also were immigrants, many of them Chinese and Irish.

Living conditions in the construction camps

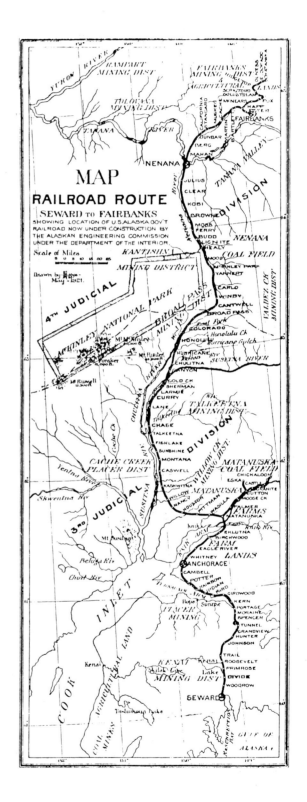

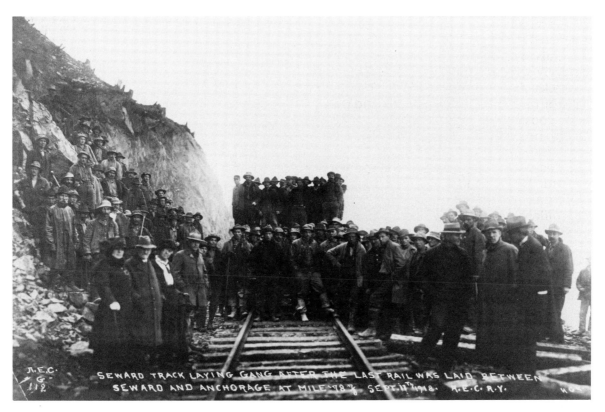

Seward track-laying gang after the last rail was put down on the stretch between Anchorage and Seward, Mile 78, Sept. 11, 1918.   AHL (Alaska RR Collection)

Crowds gather at Seward for the arrival of Interior Secretary John Barton Payne, Navy Secretary Josephus Daniels and Rear Adm. Hugh Rodman. The officials were on an inspection tour of the railroads and coal fields, July 15, 1920.   AHL (Alaska RR Collection)

Clearing track of slide debris at Mile 355.3, June 1921.
UAA (Lulu Fairbanks Collection)

Shovel and work train working south at Mile 345, July 1921.
UAA (Lulu Fairbanks Collection)

Water tank at Mile 51, October 1919.
AHL (Alaska RR Collection)

were rugged. Situated along the right-of-way, these camps were occupied summer and winter, as construction was underway year-round. The camps were supplied by trains that ran to the "end of track" and by barges working on the Knik Arm and the Tanana River. Overland freight teams also brought supplies to the camps, particularly in winter when snow-roads and frozen rivers provided ready access to construction sites.

Most of the railroad's construction was conducted on a force-account basis, in which "station men" formed partnerships as independent contractors and hired their own employees. Each employee signed a contract specifying that he would do a certain amount of work. Thus each employee in effect became a small contractor, an arrangement that seemed to work well in the construction environment along the Alaska Railroad.

At the peak of construction, in 1917, 4,500 of these small contractors were working on the line. In April of that year, however, the United States entered World War I. The numbers began to decline as men were drawn away by military service or better-paying jobs, and by 1919 the workforce was down to about 2,500.

The war brought other changes. On Jan. 31, 1918, Colonel Mears left Alaska for military service, while Commissioner Riggs resigned from the A.E.C. in May of that year upon his appointment to the governorship of Alaska. Commissioner Edes retired in 1919, and Colonel Mears returned that same year and was appointed chairman of the A.E.C. and chief engineer. Then, on Nov. 22, 1919, the railroad was reorganized, with the Seward and Anchorage divisions combined into the Southern Division, while the Fairbanks Division became the Northern Division.

Construction didn't stop for the war or for the reorganization. The line used 70-pound rail laid on untreated ties. The roadbed sometimes ran over swampy ground, and in these places temporary wooden trestles were built. In other places the line used a subfoundation of tundra; through the years, and especially during World War II, this part of the roadbed would literally wear out.

Bridging was one of the major problems that confronted the engineers—eight and one-half miles of the 470-mile main line route is spanned by bridges. Most of the original spans were made of wood, but the major river crossings—such as Hurricane Gulch and the Susitna and Tanana rivers—were spanned by steel bridges. The wooden bridges have since been replaced, although the steel structures are still in place.

Shortly after the railroad was completed the Alaska Moving Pictures Corporation used the railroad in their production "The Cheeckakos" starring Eva Gordon and Alec Luce. This photo was taken during filming at Tunnel, Mile 52.
AHFAM (Alaska RR Collection)

Looking south from Mile 91 on Turnagain Arm, March 1918.
    AHL (Alaska RR Collection)

Pile driver at work, Mile 86, Turnagain Arm.
    AHL (Alaska RR Collection)

Construction crew at work in the Turnagain Arm area, November 1917.
    AHL (Alaska RR Collection)

An example of the enormous amount of rock work needed along Turnagain Arm during the railroad's construction. Mile 100 to Mile 100.5.

AHFAM (Alaska RR Collection)

Filling grade between Potter Creek, Mile 101, and Rabbit Creek, Mile 103, along Turnagain Arm.

AHL (Alaska RR Collection)

An early day "caterpillar" freighting material from the end of the line.

AHL (Alaska RR Collection)

Building the railroad was not without danger. Three men were injured and one died at this site when a dynamite shot hung fire.

AHFAM (Alaska RR Collection)

Excursion of Anchorage baseball fans to Potter Creek, July 1917.

AHL (A.E.C. Collection)

Excursionists at Potter Creek, July 1917.

AHL (Alaska RR Collection)

COOK INLET PIONEER

AND KNIK NEWS

VOL. 1   Anchorage, Alaska, Saturday, June 5, 1915   NO. 1

Railroad Work Is Under Way At Anchorage

Anchorage, the coal terminal, presents a scene of activity, due to the construction of the big government railway system now getting fairly under way here. A slight delay has been incurred because of the shortage of certain kinds of food supplies in the government commissary, but an early steamer will relieve this situation and things will move along more vigorously and more contracts will be awarded.

In town, the chief activity is along the water front. Here pile-driver crews are working day and night shifts in erecting dockage facilities at the mouth of Ship creek. A monster barge for lighterage purposes has just been completed and launched, ready for business. A big dredger from the Panama canal zone, to dredge out the mouth of Ship creek for harbor purposes, is expected soon. Rails have been laid on a permanent grade leading from the dock site to the government storehouses and yardage areas.

The plateau north of the present business section of the town, which will be used for office buildings and residences for permanent employes, is now being cleared by a gang of twelve men under the direction of A. C. Anderson, preparatory to the beginning of construction work. The site is a most beautiful and healthful one for the purpose in view, and will be laid out with a design which comprehends both practicability and picturesqueness. At the point of the hill, overlooking the arm, the big office building will be erected, a magnificent structure, according to the plans. Beautiful Mt. McKinley, the highest mountain on the American continent, may be seen in the distance. Immediately in the rear to the east of the office building will be park grounds, in the form of a V, conforming to the contour of the plateau. Twenty foot avenues leading out from this park will reach the residences of the employes. A baseball ground and tennis court will be laid out to afford healthful recreation for the employes. Mr. Parr is the engineer in charge.

Lumber for building purposes reached here early this week from San Francisco, conveyed by the steam schooner San Ramona.

Notwithstanding the fact that there is considerable activity at

Anchorage, there is more than an adequate number of laboring men to do all that will be done in railroad work this season. Hence this newspaper takes occasion to warn those seeking work that they had best seek it elsewhere.

The Official Force

The official office and field force of the Alaskan Engineering Commission, having headquarters at Anchorage, is as follows:

Lieut. F. Mears, engineer in charge.

W. J. Fogelstrom, bridge engineer.

James O'Reilly, superintendent of construction.

C. G. Jones, assistant superintendent of construction.

K. K. Kuney, engineer in charge of locating party No. 1.

J. H. Bacon, engineer in charge of locating party No. 2.

C. R. Breck, jr., engineer in charge of locating party No. 3.

F. B. Standiford, resident engineer, in charge of division No. 1.

E. O. Archibald, resident engineer, in charge of division No. 2.

Dr. E. S. Reedy, surgeon.

D. D. Vint, draftsman.

R. D. Chase, chief clerk.

H. B. Wilkinson, accountant.

G. C. Hammond, disbursing officer.

A. M. McDermott, clerk.

M. P. Cotter, clerk.

R. P. Turner, storekeeper.

W. M. Peltier, bookkeeper.

W. R. Manning, material foreman.

H. G. Locke, harbormaster.

G. H. Remore, foreman in charge of carpenter work.

Dave McEachern, pile driver foreman.

E. A. Swift is master and Wm. Englund engineer of the government river boat Chulitna.

J. E. Pedersen is master and K. Bradland engineer of the navy launch Eklutna.

Contracts on Railway Work

The first contract let by the Commission, soon after Commissioner Mears reached Anchorage, was to David and Robertson and called for the clearing of right of way from station 3548 to 3689 inclusive, or an aggregate distance of 14,100 feet. To make this plain to the uninitiated, it should be stated that in railroad work a station is 100 feet.

Some 500 men are employed in station work, consisting of clearing right of way and grading, between Anchorage and the junction and on towards the Matanuska coal fields. The last station gang is located not to exceed 20 miles, by the railway course, from the mouth of Ship creek.

Contracts awarded to date to contractors appear below. To make the information plain, so that one may figure out just where the various contractors are employed, it may be said that where three or less figures are used in designating a specific station, that station is on the line from Anchorage to the junction. Where four figures are employed, the station is on what is termed the main road. Except in the David and Robertson contract, the contracts are let to groups of men who are equal participants and partners. The names of all not being available, the name or names of the head or heads of parties are alone given, as follows:

Contract No. 1—David & Robertson, with crew of 20 men. Station 3548 to 3689. Clearing right of way.

(Continued on page two)

Secretary Lane to Receive First Copy

Anchorage, Alaska, June 5, 1915

Hon. Franklin K. Lane,
Secretary of the Interior,
Washington, D. C.

Sir: The publishers of the Cook Inlet Pioneer wish to present to you the first copy of the first newspaper issued at Anchorage, Alaska, a prospective commercial center of importance, which owes its birth to the great Alaskan railway system now building from this point. We appreciate your wise efforts and achievements looking toward the development of our vast northern empire, so rich in natural resources and so sorely in need of the transportation facilities which the building of the government railway system will largely supply.

The Pioneer will make an effort to publish only trustworthy information concerning the huge railway project, and knowing your interest in the matter, we are placing your name on our subscription list.

Respectfully,
COOK INLET PIONEER.

Business Firms and Individuals in Local Trade

Practically all kinds of essential businesses are represented in Anchorage, and in making his rounds the Pioneer man gathered the names of the following:

In the general merchandise business are Brown & Hawkins, with J. W. Kempf in immediate charge, Finklestein & Sapiro, Carl W. Bolte, F. E. Parker and B. O. Tiedemann, A. Wilson, N. W. Pilger, E. H. Hertel, Wendler & Larson, Sheehan & Co., A. M. Laska, F. D. McCullough, Mrs. Walsh, J.M. Blase and John Bulaich & Co.

In the restaurant and bakery business are Mike Reilly, A. E. Dickson and Dave Mahoney, Jack Cronin and Carl Hortness, Mrs. Martha White, L. N. Markle, Mrs. N. Dickson, Harry Tasaki and Fred Hoyashi, R. Wufahl and R. Ramsay, Frank Zaremba, Jack Webery, P. K. Krivokapich, Geo. Johnson and J.F. Oleson, J. Hill and F. Long, Mrs. W. B. Bartholf and P.M. Lennon.

Lodging house proprietors are F. W. Redwood & Co., Mrs. Martha White, Mrs. E. Mutchler, G. E. Hudson and J. L. McNamee, Geo. Crist, A. Wilson, Mrs. Dunlap, R. G. Matheson, L. N. Markle, Wm. Murray, R. Richter, F. C. Cobbs and J. A. Holstad.

F. C. Lawrence and B. C. Nichols are the local jewelers.

In the cigar and tobacco business are R. J. Beach and Tex Jones, A. Walstrom and A. Church, Mrs. Geo. Williamson, Mrs. E. Mutchler, C. C. Bush, J.M. Sheehan and P. Burns, A. F. Frodenberg, John M. Anderson, E. J. Hertel, Roy Williamson, Rudi Marcella, V. A. Schmitz, Ore Barnhart and K. Koplan.

The local drug stores are the Northern Drug Company, V. A. Schmitz, manager, and the City Drug Store, Dr. K. A. Kyvig owner.

Oscar Anderson and Louie Jensen have a wholesale and retail meat market and J. Turner is the owner of the local fish market.

Lumber yards are conducted by R. E. McDonald, W. B. Bartholf, Herman Molen and Al. Carlson and Hussey & Richter.

Commission merchants are Hussey & Richter and R. M. McLean and C. B. Wark.

J. J. Ross and C. D. Ryther are in the painting, decorating and paper hanging business.

Transfer and storage firms are Hughes & Pedersen, with Bob

(Continued on page two)

Anchorage's first newspaper.

A typical construction camp along the railroad right-of-way.   AHL (Alaska RR Collection)

By December 1921, construction had progressed to the point that through traffic was possible from Seward to Fairbanks, although a few gaps remained. These gaps were temporarily spanned by laying tracks across ice in winter.

Two years later, the railroad was complete. On July 15, 1923, near the Nenana River bridge, the final spike—a golden one—was hammered home by President Warren G. Harding. Seward and Fairbanks were linked by a continuous line of rail.

A month later, the line's name was changed from the "Government Railroad" to "The Alaska Railroad." In addition to the 470 miles of main line, it included a 37.9-mile branch from Matanuska to the Chickaloon coal mines. In the years ahead it would be expanded further—branch lines would be built from Sutton to Eska to Jonesville, 3.8 miles; Moose Creek to Premier, 3.8 miles; from the main line at Milepost 359.2 to Healy, 4.4 miles; to the Eielson Air Force Base, 29.4 miles, and Fairbanks International Airport, 10 miles; and from the the main line to Whittier, 12.4 miles, in that stretch known as the Whittier Cutoff.

Over the years, too, parts of the line would be abandoned—in 1933, 17.9 miles of the branch line from Sutton to Chickaloon were abandoned, and in 1930 the narrow-gauge route of the former Tanana Valley Railroad from Fairbanks to Chatanika was discontinued.

With the completion of the line in 1923, both freight and passenger trains began running between Seward and Anchorage. The maintenance costs of the line, however, were very high, and the population of the territory was still very small. It was not until 1938 that the railroad became profitable and congressional appropriations were no longer needed to support it.

By that time, the railroad was beginning to need rehabilitation. After World War II, a massive rehabilitation program was undertaken—new 115-pound track was laid on treated ties and over an improved, ballasted roadbed, while wooden bridges were replaced with steel ones. In addition, new terminal buildings were constructed and sidings were extended, and some of the main line was relocated for greater safety.

The railroad faced other challenges, too. As Alaska's highway system was improved, trucks provided sharp competition for the freight business. The railroad met this competition by adopting new operating techniques and labor-saving equipment. These included the replacement of steam locomotives with diesel power, new freight and passenger rolling stock, and the establishment of car-barge and train-ship services, which linked the Alaska Railroad directly with railroads in the Lower 48.

Until April 1967, the railroad operated as an agency of the Department of the Interior. At that time, it became a bureau of the Federal Railroad Administration, part of the newly created Department of Transportation. Currently it is financed through a revolving fund, where the railroad's earnings go into its own account which can be drawn upon for capital improvements and general operating expenses. The railroad has frequently received capital and major maintenance appropriations from Congress, including millions of dollars for rebuilding after the 1964 earthquake.

The Anchorage waterfront in the winter of 1916. Note the small boats on the beach.
AHL (Alaska RR Collection)

Anchorage Harbor and the mouth of Ship Creek, October 1921.
AHFAM (Alaska RR Collection)

View of the Anchorage coal dock, June 1918.
AHL (A.E.C. Collection)

Anchorage's material and yard tracks, 1923. The power plant and machine shops are on the right and the town is in the left background.
AHFAM (Alaska RR Collection)

Coke, used in the A.E.C. iron foundry, was made at Anchorage using coal from Chickaloon, October 1919.
AHL (Alaska RR Collection)

General office of the Alaska Engineering Commission at Anchorage, August 1921.
AHL (Alaska RR Collection)

Roundhouse at Anchorage, April 1919.
UAA (Lulu Fairbanks Collection)

Mechanical department at Anchorage, 1923. Engine #606, pictured here, was a 2-6-0 Alco-Brooks that was originally built to serve the 5-foot Panama Railroad.
AHL (Alaska RR Collection)

A.E.C.'s Anchorage bunkhouses #1, 2 and 3 and mess house.
AHL (Alaska RR Collection)

Fire department at the Anchorage terminal yards, May 1919.
AHL (A.E.C. Collection)

Military guardhouse at the Anchorage terminal yards.
AHL (Alaska RR Collection)

A.E.C. employees' cottages on Government Hill. They face the Anchorage railroad yards and what is now Harvard Avenue.

Lyman Woodman, Anchorage

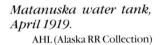

Matanuska water tank, April 1919.

AHL (Alaska RR Collection)

Station gang at camp, Mile 249. Pictured in the group is Miss E. Swensen, the only woman contractor on the railroad.

AHL (Alaska RR Collection)

TIME TABLES—THE ALASKA RAILROAD

SEWARD, ANCHORAGE, McKINLEY PARK, NENANA AND FAIRBANKS

12 Mixed Wed. Only	2 Pass'r Mon. Thur.	Miles	July 9, 1922		Elev.	1 Pass'r Wed. Sat.	11 Mixed Thur. Only
	8.00	0.0	Lv..... Seward*.....Ar		20	6 10	
	f 8 17	6.9	" ......Woodrow...... "		199	f 5 54	
	8.34	12.0	" ....Divide........ "		694	5.38	
	f 8 51	18.4	" ....Primrose....... "		457	f 5 20	
	9 05	23.3	" ......Roosevelt...... "		452	5.05	
	f 9.37	33.8	" ....Johnson....... "		486	f 4.33	
	9.55	40.0	" ....Hunter........ "		612	4.18	
	10.13	44.9	" ......Grandview...... "		1063	4 00	
	10.45	51.0	" ....Tunnel*........ "		491	3.30	
	f11.08	59.3	" ....Spencer........ "		62	f 3.02	
	f11.18	62.5	" ....Moraine........ "		37	f 2.52	
	f11.22	64.0	" ....Portage........ "		33	f 2.48	
	f11.40	70.6	" ....Kern.......... "		53	f 2.30	
	11.54	74.8	" ......Girdwood*...... "		40	2.16	
	f12.36	81.7	" ....Bird.......... "		33	f 1.54	
	f12.36	88.7	" ....Indian......... "		49	f 1.33	
	f12 51	93.5	" ....Rainbow........ "		63	f 1.19	
	f 1.12	100.6	" ....Potter......... "		32	f12.58	
	f 1 33	109.3	" ....Campbell........ "		120	f12.38	
8.50	2.15	114.3	" ....Anchorage*....... "		28	12.25	2 45
f 9.19	f 2.29	119.1	" ....Whitney........ "		222	f11.40	f 2.29
f 9.40	f 2.48	126.6	" ....Eagle River....... "		197	f11.21	f 1.59
f10.13	f 3.13	136.3	" ......Birchwood*...... "		92	f10.56	f 1.29
f10.40	f 3.29	141.9	" ....Eklutna........ "		50	f10.40	f 1.07
11.05	3.55	150.7	" ....Matanuska*....... "		36	10.20	12 40
	4.19	159.8	" ....Wasilla*......... "		339	9.53	
	f 4.35	166.5	" ....Pittman......... "		300	f 9.35	
	f 4.56	174.9	" ....Houston........ "		246	f 9.14	
	f 5.12	181.3	" ....Nancy.......... "		236	f 8.58	
	5.28	185.7	" ....Willow.......... "		232	8.47	
	f 5.48	193.9	" ......Kashwitna...... "		236	f 8.22	
	f 6 09	202.3	" ....Caswell......... "		246	f 8.01	
	6.28	209.3	" ....Montana........ "		282	7.45	
	f 6.43	215.3	" ....Sunshine....... "		328	f 7.27	
	f 6.57	221.3	" ....Fishlake........ "		310	f 7.13	
	7.14	226.7	" ....Talkeetna*....... "		354	6.58	
	f 7.37	236.2	" ....Chase.......... "		462	f 6.33	
	f 7.54	242.6	" ....Lane........... "		492	f 6.16	
	8.25	248.3	" ....Curry*.......... "		546	5.50	
	f 8.48	257.0	" ....Sherman........ "		621	f 5.21	
	f 9 06	263.5	" ....Gold Creek....... "		731	f 5.02	
	9 24	268.4	" ....Canyon......... "		879	f 4.47	
	f 9 42	273.9	" ....Chulitna........ "		1280	f 4.29	
	10 11	281.4	" ....Hurricane....... "		1688	4.00	
	f10 40	288.7	" ....Honolulu........ "		1456	f 3.36	
	f11.12	297.1	" ....Colorado........ "		1954	f 3.04	
	12.05	304.3	" ....Broad Pass*....... "		2127	2.35	
	f12.38	312.5	" ....Summit......... "		2337	f 1.38	
	f 1.06	319.5	" ....Cantwell........ "		2212	f 1.10	
	1.35	326.7	" ....Windy*.......... "		2056	12.41	
	f 2.06	334.4	" ....Yanert......... "		1965	f12.10	
	f 2.34	341.5	" ....Carlo.......... "		1965	f11.42	
	3.01	347.9	" .....McKinley Park*..... "		1732	11.17	
	f 3.23	353.2	" ....Moody......... "		1491	f10.55	
	3.55	358.2	" ....Healy*......... "		1368	10.35	
	f 4.10	363.3	" ....Lignite......... "		1176	f10.13	
	f 4.35	371.6	" ....Ferry.......... "		1006	f 9.52	
	f 4 43	374.2	" ....Moss.......... "		960	f 9.45	
4 Mixed Tu. Fr. Th. Sa.	6 Motor Mo.We.					5 Motor Mo.We. Th. Sa.	3 Mixed Tu. Fr.
	f 5.04	381.2	" ....Browne......... "		810	f 9.28	
	f 5.23	387.2	" ....Kobe.......... "		705	f 8.56	
	f 5.44	394.2	" ....Clear.......... "		537	f 8.34	
	f 6.09	401.3	" ....Julius.......... "		433	8.00	
1 30	12 45	6.45	411.5	" ....Nenana*......... "	362	11.55	12 30
2 10	1.00	Arrive Tu. Fr.	412.9	" ....North Nenana....... "	367	Leave Tu. Fr.	12.06
f 2.24	f 1.18	417.7	" ....Mahon......... "		370	f11.12	f11.43
2 40	f 1.34	423.1	" ....Berg.......... "		368	f10.56	f11.25
2.56	1.53	429.3	" ....Dunbar........ "		368	10.37	11.09
f 3.25	f 2.07	433.2	" ....California........ "		397	f10.24	f10.46
f 3 43	f 2.19	436.7	" ....Standard........ "		406	f10.13	f10.32
f 3.59	f 2.36	442.1	" ....Muskeg......... "		433	f 9.56	f10.16
4 15	f 2.51	14 Mixed Mo. Th.	446.7	" ....Cache.......... "	456	f 9.41	f 1.12
4 36	3.02	451.5	" ....Martin......... "		510	9.25	9.35
5 04	3 20	455.5	" ....Bartlett........ "		542	9.12	9.06
5 25	3.37	3 05	460.2	" ....Happy......... "	609	8.30	8 56 8 38
5.34	3 45	3 14	462.7	" ....Ester.......... "	489	8 19	8.19
5.50	4.00	3 30	467.5	Ar.......Fairbanks*.......Lv	448	8.00	8.30 8.00

* Telegraph station.
f Flag stop.

EQUIPMENT—Trains 1 and 2.

Observation Parlor-Buffet Car Seward and Nenana.
Sleeping Car Anchorage and Nenana.

MATANUSKA, SUTTON AND CHICKALOON

12-22 Mixed Wed. Only	Miles	July 9, 1922	Elev.	21-11 Mixed Thur. Only
8 50	0.0	Lv.....Anchorage*.....Ar	28	2 45
11.05	36.4	Ar.....Matanuska*.....Lv	36	12 40
11 20	0.0	Lv.....Matanuska*.....Ar	36	12 05
11.50	6.5	" ....Palmer........, "	256	11.48
12.45	13.2	" ......Moose Creek...... "	340	11 27
1.05	18.9	" ....Sutton.........Lv	448	11.05
	2.7	Ar..........Eska..........Lv	983	
	2.9	Ar.......Jonesville.......Lv	837	
3.00	18.9	Lv.........Sutton.........Ar	448	8.30
f 3.09	22.4	" ....Granite......... "	520	f 8.23
f 3 21	29.8	" ....Castle.......... "	696	f 8.04
3.50	37.7	Ar......Chickaloon*......Lv	929	7.40

Eska Branch—Sutton to Eska and Jonesville. Freight service only, passengers not carried on trains operating on this branch.

HAPPY AND CHATANIKA

13-24 Mixed Mon. Thur.	26 Ex. Motor Tues.	Miles	July 9, 1922	Elev.	25 Ex. Motor Tues. Fri.	23-14 Mixed Mon. Thur.
8.00	8.30	0 0	Lv.....Fairbanks*.....Ar	448	3 00	3.30
8 30	8.56	7.3	Ar.........Happy.........Lv	609	2.37	3.05
8.33	8.56	0.0	Lv.........Happy.........Ar	609	2.37	3.02
f 8.49	f 9.13	4.1	" ....McNears......... "	624	f 2.19	f 2.46
9.15	9.35	10.7	" ....Fox.......... "	754	1.59	2.18
9.55	9.55	13.2	" ....Gilmore*......... "	883	1.43	1.57
10.24	10.21	18.8	" ....Scrafford........ "	1430	1.15	1.25
10.34	10.31	21.7	" ....Ridgetop........ "	1087	1.01	1.12
11 05	10.53	26.4	" ....Olnes......... "	609	12.35	12.45
11.38	11.07	29.6	" ....Eldorado........ "	610	12.22	12.24
11.50	11.20	31.9	Ar.......Chatanika.......Lv	654	12.10	12.10

* Telegraph station. f Flag stop.

GENERAL INFORMATION

Not Responsible. The Alaska Railroad is not responsible for errors in time tables, inconvenience or damage resulting from delayed trains or failure to make connections; schedules herein are subject to change without notice.

Buy Tickets. Passengers should purchase tickets before boarding trains.

Children under 5 years of age, free, when accompanied by parent or guardian; 5 years of age and under 12, one-half fare; 12 years of age or over, full fare.

Adjustment of Fares. In cases of dispute with Conductors or Agents, pay the fare required, take receipt and communicate with The Alaska Railroad, General Office, Anchorage, Alaska.

Redemption of Tickets. Tickets unused, or partly used, will be redeemed under tariff regulations at proper value.

Baggage Maximums. No single piece of baggage exceeding 250 pounds in weight, or 72 inches in greatest dimension, or single shipment exceeding $2,500.00 in value will be checked. Free allowances subject to tariff stipulations as to contents, weight, value and size.

Liability Limited. Excess value to be declared and paid for at time of checking.

Bicycles (not Motorcycles), Baby Carriages, Dogs and Guns are transported in baggage cars subject to tariff regulations.

Lost Articles should be inquired for through The Alaska Railroad, General Office Anchorage, Alaska, or nearest agent.

No Responsibility is Assumed for unchecked articles left in stations or cars

Telegraph Service. Stations indicated with * are telegraph stations handling telegrams to any part of the world.

Express Service handled by the American Railway Express Co. as a part of its national system of express transportation.

SAFETY FIRST

Do not leave your grips and packages in the car aisle. Some one may fall over them.

Place your suit cases or grips in the racks so they will be secure and not fall on some one's head.

Keep your arms and head inside the car windows.

Never board or leave a moving train. Wait until it stops.

Look where you step. Take no chances.

Do not allow children to run about while car is in motion. Injury to them may result.

Do not cross the tracks without looking both ways.

Do not stand on platform of coaches while they are in motion.

Do not stand on or too near the track.

Bold face figures indicate P. M. time; light face A. M. time.

Extra gang #3 waiting for the dinner bell at Mile 232 near Talkeetna, July 1919.
AHFAM (Alaska RR Collection)

A deep cut through gravelly soil, June 1921. Note the horse and the tripods for a telegraph line.
AHL (Alaska RR Collection)

Steel gang at Mile 288.5, August 1921.
AHL (Alaska RR Collection)

Interior of the district engineer's office, Dead Horse district headquarters, March 1918.
AHL (Alaska RR Collection)

Survey party at Fourth of July Creek above "Colorado" milepost at the entrance to Broad Pass, June 1923.
AHFAM (Alaska RR Collection)

Soil conditions were a constant problem for construction workers, especially in the Nenana River Canyon. This view looks north from the top of tunnel #2, June 27, 1921.
UAA (Lulu Fairbanks Collection)

Locomotive #6, formerly used in Panama, being pulled uphill by horses, near Healy, 1920. The locomotive was to be used south of the Nenana River Canyon.
AHFAM (Alaska RR Collection)

Steel viaduct and wood trestle across Riley Creek at Mount McKinley Park, winter of 1921-22.
AHFAM (Alaska RR Collection)

Steel gang at Mile 460 near Fairbanks, October 1917.
AHFAM (Alaska RR Collection)

Construction-crew camp at Nenana, June 1917.

AHL (Alaska RR Collection)

A combination freight and passenger train leaving the Nenana station for Anchorage, May 1922.

AHFAM (Alaska RR Collection)

The North Nenana Limited *loading freight and passengers on the ice of the Tanana River, at Nenana, 1920.*

AHFAM (Alaska RR Collection)

Healy station and railroad buildings, Mile 359, November 1922.
AHL (Alaska RR Collection)

Suntrana coal mines, November 1922.
AHL (Alaska RR Collection)

Eska coal mining area and railroad complex, July 1921.
AHFAM (Alaska RR Collection)

Secretary of the Interior John B. Payne and Secretary of the Navy Josephus Daniels at the end of steel, Mile 243, on an inspection trip, July 16, 1920.　　AHL (Alaska RR Collection)

The first train to run from Seward arrived at Nenana on Feb. 5, 1922.　　AHFAM (Alaska RR Collection)

President Warren G. Harding driving the golden spike at North Nenana, July 15, 1923. The spike completed the rail link between the port town of Seward and the interior town of Fairbanks, and was the finishing touch on what at that point was the greatest construction project in Alaska's history.   AHFAM (Alaska RR Collection)

President Harding in the cab of engine #618, the engine that pulled the excursion train on his Alaskan visit, July 1923.   AHFAM (Alaska RR Collection)

Otto F. Ohlson, general manager of the railroad, poses in front of the Curry Hotel with his Dodge railmobile, 1938. Ohlson guided the railroad through much of its early development, including the World War II years. His tenure ran from 1928 to 1945. AHFAM

Administrative staff of the Alaska Railroad in 1944. Otto Ohlson is sitting at the desk.
AHFAM (Alaska RR Collection)

BUFFET CAR, A. E. C.

MENU

❖

Oranges - .25   Bananas - .25   Apple Sauce - .25   Baked Apples - .35
Peaches - .35   Grapes - .35   Pears - .35   Grape Fruit - .35

BREAKFAST FOODS

Uncle Sam Breakfast Food - .25;   Krumbles - 25;   Shredded Wheat - .25
Post Toasties - .25
Grape-Nuts - .25   Corn Flakes - .25   Puffed Rice - .20   Dry Toast - .20
Buttered Toast - .20 — Dipped Toast - .20   Snails - .20   Doughnuts - .20
Drop Cakes - .20   Coffee Cake - .20   Apple turn-over - .20   Hot Buns - .20
Bread and Butter - .20   French Toast and Preserves - 1.00   Jelly - .25
Preserves or Jam - .25

DISHES COOKED TO ORDER

Ham and Eggs	$1 00	Bacon and Eggs	$1 00
Fried Ham	1 00	Fried Bacon	1 00
Minced Ham and Eggs	1 00	Ham Omelet	1 00
Bacon Omelet	1 00	Onion Omelet	1 00
Jelly Omelet	1 00	Tomato Omelet	1 00
Spanish Omelet	1 25	Oyster Omelet	1 25
Fried Eggs (3)	1 00	Shirred Eggs (3)	1 00
Fried Eggs (2)	75	Shirred Eggs (2)	75
Scrambled Eggs (2)	75	Plain Omelet	1 00
Scrambled Eggs (3)	1 00	Cheese Omelet	1 00

WE SERVE STRICTLY FRESH EGGS

Coffee Per Cup - .10   Chocolate - .15   Cocoa - .15   Pot Tea - .25
Pot of Fresh Made Coffee - .25
Matanuska Fried Potatoes to Order - .15

" WE BUY THE BEST "

Cigars — Cigarettes   Fruits, Candies and Nuts.

BREAKFAST 8 A. M. to 9:30 A. M.   LUNCHEON 11 to 2 P. M.

DINNER 4:30 To

J. CASY McDANNEL,
Contractor

— — — — — — ❖ — — — — — — —

Menu from 1920.
UAA (C.M. Andrews Collection)

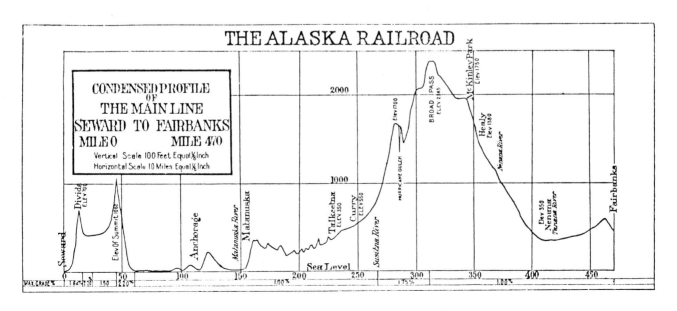

-41-

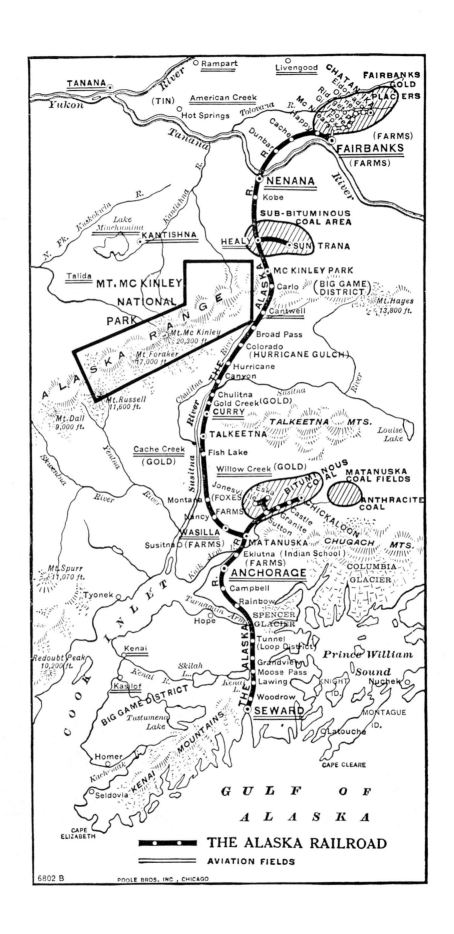

THE ALASKA RAILROAD
AVIATION FIELDS

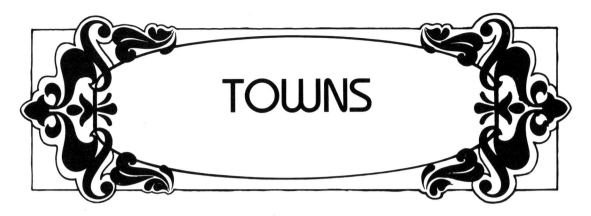

TOWNS

Seward

At the north end of Resurrection Bay, and almost completely surrounded by mountains, is the southern terminus of the railroad—Seward. Like many of the towns along the Alaska Railroad, it really didn't get its start until the railroad came through early in the 20th century.

In the late 18th century, Russian naval officers had christened the bay Resurrection, or Sunday Bay, and had established a shipyard there. Yet it wasn't until 1884 that Frank Lowell, a trader from Kodiak, settled in the vicinity, becoming the first American to do so. Not until the turn of the century did the settlement amount to much.

In June 1902, a survey party landed at the site of Seward and began to lay out a route for the Alaska Central Railroad. Shortly afterward, in July 1903, the townsite was surveyed and named for William H. Seward, who, as U.S. secretary of state, had negotiated the purchase of Alaska in 1867.

With the arrival of the Alaska Central Railroad, a wharf was constructed at Seward and streets laid out. But the railroad, and its successor, the Alaska Northern, never extended more than 70 miles from Seward. Eventually it fell on hard times and operations ceased. Soon, however, the Alaska Railroad was born.

When news reached Seward in August 1915 that it would be the southern terminus of the railroad, a new kind of stampede occurred, akin to the gold stampedes of earlier days. Real estate prices in Seward shot up, lots changed hands overnight, new stores opened, and steamers arrived carrying scores of men who were looking for work. As temporary headquarters of the Alaska Railroad, the town boomed.

An early view of Seward's dock and Main Street.   UAA (Col. Mears Collection)

Seward's Main Street, July 15, 1920.

Seward, with its location at Mile 0, would become an important town along the railroad. This photo, showing the old station on the right, was taken in the 1940s.

With the completion of the railroad in 1923, however, and the removal to Anchorage of the railroad's headquarters, Seward settled down to a steady growth as the railroad's southern terminus as well as its only deepwater port.

Then, in 1943, the opening of the Whittier Cutoff reduced the importance of the port of Seward. Use of the port dropped further after the war, and today the town is no longer totally dependent upon the railroad. Seward may not be the boomtown it was earlier in the century, but today it has a more diverse economy.

Anchorage

The flats along Ship Creek were already in use before the railroad came through and before the town of Anchorage existed. Steam and sailing vessels in the Cook Inlet used the area for an anchorage, the use that would give the town its name.

Gold discoveries spawned the first settlement in the area. Gold was discovered along Turnagain Arm south of the flats in 1888, and mines at Girdwood and Crow Creek went into full production. While some prospectors rushed to the gold strikes at

Nome and Fairbanks, others settled at the gold town of Knik, across Knik Arm from the present city center.

There were a few settlers on the site of present-day Anchorage when the railroad survey came through in 1914. Ship Creek became the field headquarters for the A.E.C. in 1914 and a few log buildings were constructed for the staff. On April 10, 1915, President Wilson, by executive order, announced the selection of the western route for the Alaska Railroad, and the A.E.C. found that its Ship Creek headquarters, which were located not quite halfway between Seward and Fairbanks, was an ideal site to launch rail construction toward the Matanuska coalfields. Ships carrying supplies also could sail up Cook Inlet and lie at anchorage in Knik Arm.

The area around the flats took on the appearance of the former gold rush towns of interior Alaska and the Yukon. Ship Creek became known as "Tent City," with thousands of squatters staking their tents below the plateau now called Government Hill.

Commissioner Mears arrived in the new tent city on April 26, 1915, and immediately ordered preparation of a townsite plan to bring some order to

Anchorage was little more than a tent city when this photo was taken in 1915.   AHFAM

the chaos he saw. Andrew Christensen, chief of the Alaska field division of the General Land Office, soon laid out a town of 1,400 lots, with approximately 50 by 140 feet for each lot. Land was set aside for schools, parks, and government buildings, while the tent city was removed to make room for the proposed railroad yards.

On July 10, 1915, a public auction was held to sell the lots to the highest bidders. Commercial lots in the downtown area fetched the highest prices, while residential lots sold for much less money. Between 1,000 and 3,000 people attended the auction. The town, soon to be formally named Anchorage, was firmly established.

For the next five years the A.E.C. managed the new town. On Nov. 23, 1920, the A.E.C. turned the town over to the newly incorporated city and its new city council. The railroad, however, still kept a strong presence in the town that it had spawned. With the increased importance of Anchorage as a construction and administrative center, the railroad moved its main administrative offices to Anchorage from Seward on Jan. 1, 1917. Today Anchorage is still the general headquarters for the Alaska Railroad.

Main Street of the "tent city" along Ship Creek in July 1915. A public auction was held on July 10 to sell lots, formally establishing the new town of Anchorage.

AHFAM (Sidney Laurence Photo)

As in other towns along the railroad, the U.S. government auctioned off lots in Anchorage to foster settlement. In the first sale at Anchorage, the first lot sold for $825. AHL (Alaska RR Collection)

New 12-foot concrete sidewalks in Anchorage, about 1920.

AHL (Alaska RR Collection)

Anchorage was beginning to resemble a town when this photo was taken in 1917. The view is of Fifth Avenue, looking east from L Street. AHL (Alaska RR Collection)

The Government Hill housing project above Anchorage's railroad complex, December 1947. The A.E.C. built its first employee cottages on Government Hill in 1915. The area was annexed to the city in 1946. AHFAM (Alaska RR Collection)

Nenana

Nenana originally was an Indian village on the south bank of the Tanana River, at the point where the Tanana and the Nenana rivers join. The Tanana River is the largest tributary of the Yukon River, which was a main artery for travel and freight earlier this century.

The Alaska Railroad crosses the Tanana River at the town of Nenana. Thus the town was a very important transfer point for freight from the railroad that was to be put on riverboats and delivered to towns up and down the Yukon River in both Alaska and the Yukon. With the coming of the airplane, river boat traffic fell off; however, winter supplies destined for villages still move down the Tanana and on the Yukon throughout the summer months.

Nenana, at the railroad's crossing of the Tanana River, would develop into a major town along the new railbelt. Top: Main Street, with the new railroad station under construction. Bottom: The waterfront, July 1916.
AHL (Alaska RR Collection)

Fairbanks

Seward, Anchorage, and other towns along the railbelt were founded as a direct result of railroad construction, but Fairbanks was a town long before the railroad came through.

Fairbanks' history began with a gold strike in 1902 by Felix Pedro. The gold in the area generally was buried under 80 to 100 feet of muck and gravel, and mining it required large-scale equipment rather than the picks and shovels individual prospectors had used in earlier gold strikes. For this reason, the mining area and the town grew in a more orderly and contained fashion than the earlier gold rush towns of Dawson and Nome.

Because of the need for large-scale equipment, mining in the Fairbanks area languished until 1923, when the Alaska Railroad was completed. With the arrival of the railroad, heavy equipment could be brought in much more easily, and Fairbanks took on new importance as a mining center. Mine production has since slowed, but the city is still the northern terminus of the railroad as well as the economic focal point for all of interior Alaska.

Other towns either got their start or grew because of the railroad. These include Palmer, Wasilla, Talkeetna, Chickaloon, Eska, Curry and Healy. Some of these towns have disappeared or dropped in population due to the ups and downs of the region's coal-mining industry and the resulting fluctuations in coal tonnage carried by the Alaska Railroad.

Wasilla, at Mile 159. Top: June 20, 1917, the day the town lots were put up for sale. Bottom: Station and other early buildings, Oct. 11, 1918.
AHL (Alaska RR Collection)

Eska, a coal-mining town, in May 1919.
AHL (Alaska RR Collection)

Cottages at the new townsite of Emery, on Eska Creek.
AHL (Alaska RR Collection)

Commission Avenue, Talkeetna, when tents made up most of the town.
AHL (Alaska RR Collection)

The new townsite of Talkeetna, at Mile 226.7.
AHFAM (Alaska RR Collection)

The newly built town of Chickaloon. Middle: October, 1918. Bottom: July, 1921.
AHL (Alaska RR Collection)

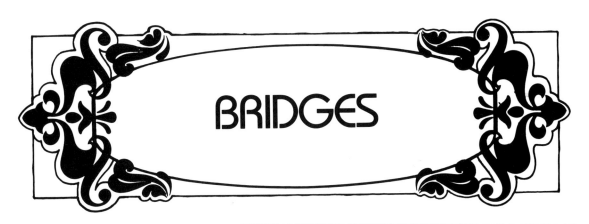

BRIDGES

Two completed, all-wood spans across the Matanuska River, August 1916. Notice the "rubberneck" open air observation car on the left span.   AHL (Alaska RR Collection)

During World War I, guards were placed at the railroad's major bridge to protect against sabotage. Pictured is the Eagle River trestle bridge at Mile 127.5, May 1918.

AHL (Alaska RR Collection)

American Bridge Co. crews working on an assembled part of truss span for the Tanana River Bridge, September 1922.

AHL (Alaska RR Collection)

View of the Tanana River Bridge and the town of Nenana, Aug. 22, 1922.

AHL (Alaska RR Collection)

Trestle approach to the Tanana River Bridge at Nenana, July 30, 1922. This was the last major bridge project on the railroad and it provided a final link on the north-south route.

AHL (Alaska RR Collection)

Tanana River Bridge, looking east, Jan. 5, 1923.   AHL (Alaska RR Collection)

The completed Tanana River Bridge at Nenana, February 1923. The falsework piling is frozen in the ice.
AHFAM (Alaska RR Collection)

The Susitna River bridge, located about halfway between Anchorage and Fairbanks, May 1921.
UAA (Lulu Fairbanks Collection)

The reconstruction of bridge #75, October 1919.

UAA (Col. Mears Collection)

Susitna River bridge site at Mile 264, Sept. 15, 1920.

AHL (Alaska RR Collection)

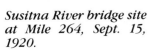

-56-

South end of the tramway spanning Hurricane Gulch, 1921.   UAA (Col. Mears Collection)

The most expensive and difficult bridge project on the railroad was the construction of a span across Hurricane Gulch at Mile 281.4. An aerial tramway had to be strung across the gulch, and construction was undertaken from both sides. This photo was taken during the early days of the project, in March 1921.   UAA (Col. Mears Collection)

Nearing the completion of the Hurricane Gulch bridge, Aug. 8, 1921.

Men of the American Bridge Co. crew at the Hurricane Gulch bridge site, Aug. 16, 1921.
AHFAM (Alaska RR Collection)

Turnagain Arm was a major challenge to the bridge builders. They had to deal with large fluctuations in tides and they constantly battled against snow and ice. Pictured is a trestle at Mile 88 during the construction phase of the railroad.   AHFAM

Another major area of bridge construction was the Nenana River Canyon, where many of the old wooden bridges had to be replaced with steel spans. The unusual soil conditions caused earth to slide downhill, thus weakening or destroying the wooden bridge piers. These bridges were replaced in 1948.   AHFAM (Alaska RR Collection)

Top: Early photo of the "Loop." Bottom: Opening day of the new alignment on Nov. 6, 1951. The new route eliminated costly annual repairs to five loop bridges, as well as a snowshed and one tunnel. AHFAM (Alaska RR Collection)

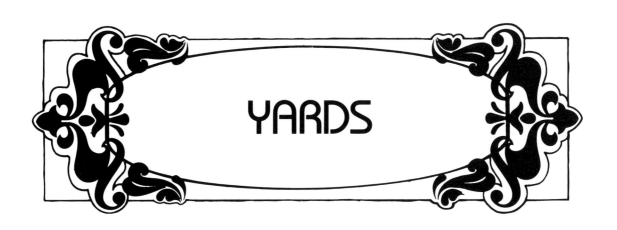

YARDS

Roundhouse at Anchorage, April 1919. The building could handle 12 locomotives.
AHL (AEC Collection)

Material and equipment that had been shipped from Panama stored at the Anchorage yards.
AHL (AEC Collection)

Anchorage railroad yards, offices and commissary department, as seen from E Street. The new freight shed and depot are in the foreground.   AHL (AEC Collection)

Office building and soldiers' quarters at the Anchorage yards, May 9, 1920.
          AHL (AEC Collection)

Machine shop and powerhouse at the Anchorage yards, 1920.   AHL (AEC Collection)

Material yard and carpenters' and machine shops, Anchorage yards, May 1, 1919.

AHL (AEC Collection)

Roundhouse at the Anchorage yards, Nov. 17, 1948. View is from the water tower.
AHFAM (Alaska RR Collection)

The Fairbanks yard complex in 1960.
AHFAM (Alaska RR Collection)

The Fairbanks yard complex with the city in the background, 1949.
AHFAM (Alaska RR Collection)

STATIONS

The first train to leave the new depot at Anchorage, November 1916.   AHL (AEC Collection)

Anchorage's first depot, built in 1915.   AHL (Alaska AEC Collection)

The Tanana Valley Railroad station at Fairbanks.
AHL (Alaska RR Collection)

Fairbanks station built by the A.E.C. to replace the Tanana Valley station. This is a World War II-era photo.
Henry Hunt, Baytown, Texas

Train #5, the AuRoRa, waits at the Fairbanks depot before starting its run to Anchorage, 1957. The old depot was built in the early 1900s for the Tanana Valley Railroad and was located at the north end of the Cushman Street bridge. It was replaced in 1960 by the present depot.
AHFAM (Alaska RR Collection)

-68-

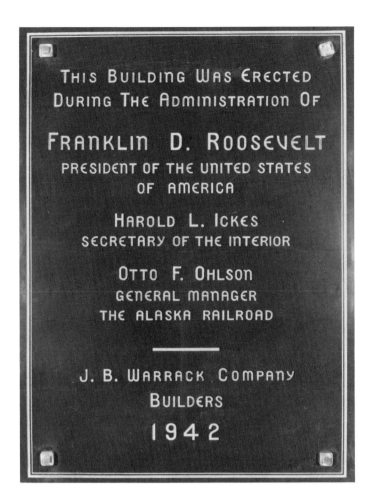

THIS BUILDING WAS ERECTED
DURING THE ADMINISTRATION OF

FRANKLIN D. ROOSEVELT
PRESIDENT OF THE UNITED STATES
OF AMERICA

HAROLD L. ICKES
SECRETARY OF THE INTERIOR

OTTO F. OHLSON
GENERAL MANAGER
THE ALASKA RAILROAD

J. B. WARRACK COMPANY
BUILDERS
1942

The new depot and general office for the railroad opened on Sept. 15, 1942. The old depot, shown at left, was soon removed. Through the years, several additions have been made to the newer building.
AHFAM

The Seward station, 1936.   AHFAM (Alaska RR Collection)

The Wasilla depot, 1919.   AHL (Alaska RR Collection)

Station and warehouse between Seward and Portage at Lawing, Mile 23.3, 1930s.
AHFAM (Alaska RR Collection)

Old passenger and freight cars served as stations along the railroad. Middle: Portage. Bottom: Moose Pass, 1951.
AHFAM (Alaska RR Collection)

Dormitory, hotel and depot at
Healy, Mile 358, in 1956.
AHFAM (Alaska RR Collection)

Cantwell's railroad facilities.
UAA (Reul Griffin Collection)

McKinley Park station, 1938.
AHFAM (Alaska RR Collection)

RIVER BOATS

Although its main interest was in providing rail service, the Alaska Railroad was extensively involved in river transportation during the first decades of its operation. River transportation initially was needed to construct the line; after the railroad's completion, the company operated its own river boat service.

Material for the railroad's construction was hauled north by oceangoing ships, and then taken by the trains of the White Pass and Yukon Route to St. Michael and Whitehorse. From there, the construction supplies were loaded on river boats operated by the Northern Commercial Co. and the American Yukon Navigation Co., which had consolidated river boat service on the Yukon River over the years and was a subsidiary of the White Pass railroad.

The boats unloaded at the native village Nenana, located on the Tanana River 192 miles above its confluence with the Yukon. A freight facility at Nenana was established to handle the supplies for the construction of that part of the railroad that lay north of Milepost 348 (in the vicinity of present-day Mount McKinley National Park).

In 1921, however, during the sixth year of railroad construction, the American Yukon Navigation Co. terminated river boat service below Fort Yukon. This created an economic hardship for the region's residents as well as hindered the railroad's construction.

The U.S. Department of Interior, after trying to persuade the navigation company to resume operations, authorized the Alaska Railroad in 1923 to begin its own river boat operation. Passenger, mail

Launching the Betty M *at Anchorage on Aug. 1, 1917. One of the small river boats used during the construction days.*
AHFAM (Alaska RR Collection)

Early day river boats that were used at the time of the railroad's construction.

Top: AHL (Alaska RR Collection)
Middle and bottom: AHFAM (Alaska RR Collection)

and freight service was inaugurated on the Tanana and Yukon rivers between Nenana and Holy Cross, a distance of 642 miles. In 1925 the route was extended to Marshall, 132 miles below Holy Cross on the Yukon, and in 1946 it was extended still farther to Circle.

The railroad began its river operations with two boats, the *Gen. Jeff C. Davis* and the *Gen. J.W. Jacobs.* These had been operated on the Yukon River by the U.S. Army and were turned over to the railroad in 1922 after the Army had abandoned most of its military installations in Alaska.

The two river boats hauled supplies for the railroad's construction, and with the completion of the railroad in 1923, the railroad used them for its commercial river boat service. When these boats were retired, other boats were added: the steamer. *Alice* was put into service in 1929 and retired in 1953; The *Nenana,* another steamer, was built by

the ARR in 1933 and taken out of service in 1956 and subsequently donated to Alaskaland in Fairbanks where it is now on display. Other boats included the *Yukon* and the *Barry K,* used in the late 1940s, as well as a number of barges that were used to haul freight.

The river boat passenger service eventually met competition from commercial airlines and highway use, and it was discontinued in 1949, while the mail service had halted a year earlier. By 1953, steamboats no longer plied the waters of the Yukon and Tanana rivers.

In March 1955, the railroad leased the remaining barge freight service to the B and R Tug and Barge Co. B and R turned over its interests to the Yutana Barge Lines, which continue to carry freight today on the Yukon and Tanana rivers. In 1980, ARR sold all its equipment to Yutana, and leased the land to the city of Nenana.

Railroad dock at Nenana on the Tanana River, Oct. 1, 1920. River boats picked up supplies here to service towns along the Yukon and Tanana rivers.

AHFAM (Alaska RR Collection)

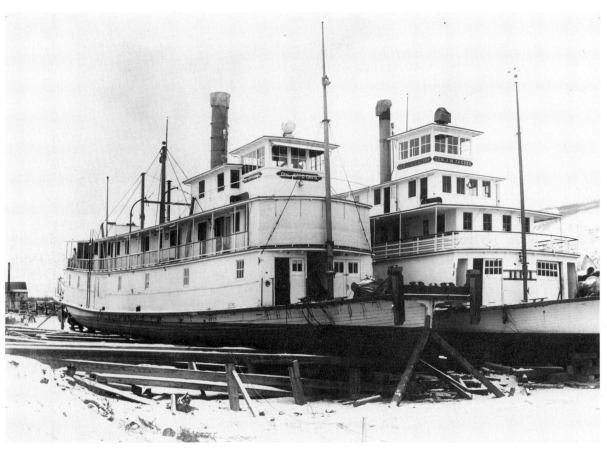

The Gen. Jeff C. Davis *and the* Gen. J.W. Jacobs. *Formerly operated by the U.S. Army, these two river boats were acquired by the railroad in 1922 to service towns along the Yukon River.*

Railroad steamboats Alice *and* Barry K *in winter quarters at Nenana, 1948.*

The Nenana *is shown taking on cargo at Nenana for transport downriver to Galena, World War II era.*

The Yukon, *docked at Nenana, unloads mules that were used in a short-lived railroad survey of interior Alaska during World War II. The railroad was proposed to run west from the Alaska Railroad to Teller on the Seward Peninsula and east into the Yukon to connect with Prince George, British Columbia. The insert is of Captain Howard of the* Yukon.

UAA (Eddy Davis Collection)

The Tanana, *a vessel of the Yutana Barge Lines, at Nenana. It was built in 1953 and is the largest boat on the river.*

AHFAM (Alaska RR Collection)

Interior of the original
McKinley Park Hotel.   Alaska RR

During the war, soldiers came
to the McKinley Park Hotel for
rest and recreation.
U.S. Army Military History Institute

Colorful brochures were produced each year to lure tourists to Alaska and the use of the railroad.

WINTER CONDITIONS

Winter weather in Alaska, of course, can be brutal, and it can paralyze any form of transportation that is not equipped with extensive maintenance services. The Alaska Railroad had, and still has, an elaborate system of snow removal and other services to keep the line open during the winter months.

The railroad's southern terminus, at Seward on Resurrection Bay, is located at a port that is free of ice all year round. Just north of Seward, however, the railroad stretches 64.2 miles through the mountainous Kenai Peninsula where it is subject to very deep snow.

The snow on the peninsula can fall 10 to 15 feet deep during the course of a winter. When the Kenai portion of the line was in daily operation, huge rotary snowplows were used almost constantly from December to April. Avalanches were another hazard. Snowsheds were built over the tracks in areas of high snow concentration and until about 1935, when bulldozers were used to clear away the slides, the snow was removed by hand tools and explosives. Sometimes it would take over 100 men, working with pick and shovel, to clear away a snowslide.

The 50-mile stretch of railroad along Turnagain Arm to Anchorage also historically has presented formidable obstacles. Avalanches were, and still are, a common problem along the steep mountain walls. Ice buildup on the roadbed also hampers operations. The ice results from bank seepage and small creeks that freeze during extreme cold weather. Extra caution is needed to check the tracks ahead of the trains.

Another area of heavy snow buildup occurs from Anchorage to Canyon, near the south entrance to Broad Pass. This area has an average snowfall of between two to five feet, while winter temperatures range from 0 degrees to 50 below and strong winds pile the snow into deep, hard-packed drifts. V-type snow spreaders are used to remove snow in this area, and they are in operation almost continuously.

Moose herds also have been a winter problem for the railroad. Deep snow hinders the animal's ability to run, and moose have climbed onto the cleared tracks to escape the menace of wolf packs. Hundreds of moose have been killed each year and countless delays caused by their rambles along the tracks.

When frost sinks deep into the ground, the railroad is plagued by frost heaves. Where the ground is insulated with grass, leaves and loose snow, the frost generally penetrates only two or three feet. But where the snow is compacted or has been removed, such as along the railroad right-of-way, the frost can penetrate to depths of five and 10 feet, depending on the structure of the sub-deposits. The moisture in the soil then freezes and expands, causing heaves. These can bend or buckle the tracks or damage bridge abutments and pilings. The railroad has fought this problem by using shims to level the track.

A problem of the opposite nature has occurred in the Nenana River Canyon, where part of the roadbed runs over permafrost. When the railroad was constructed, gravel and glacial deposits that had thawed were removed and some of the natural drainage channels were altered. This created new thaw areas, especially in the gumbo-filled hollows, thereby causing long sections of the subgrade to settle and slide toward the river.

The spring thaw presents its own set of problems. Ice jams and flooding of the tracks has occurred in a number of places, especially along the Susitna River section between Milepost 225 and 263. During spring breakup, the thawing slopes of glacial moraines sometimes come tumbling down in mud slides.

In 1953, the railroad completed an extensive rehabilitation program that lessened some of these problems. New 115-pound rail and new treated ties were laid on a well-ballasted and widened roadbed. In addition, the railroad constructed better drainage facilities and replaced old wooden bridges with new steel structures. These improvements greatly increased the railroad's efficiency of operations and reduced its annual maintenance costs.

Snowslide at Mile 72, Nov. 29, 1918. At the time, snow-removal equipment was rather primitive and hand removal was frequently employed.　　　　　　AHL (Alaska RR Collection)

Passengers from Anchorage are shown walking over snowslide at Mile 72 to catch a train for Seward on the other side, Nov. 29, 1918.

AHL (Alaska RR Collection)

Many snowsheds had to be built over the tracks, especially in the vicinity of Turnagain Arm. Pictured is a shed at Mile 73.5 in October 1919.

AHL (Alaska RR Collection)

Inside view of snowshed.

AHL (Alaska RR Collection)

Railroad workers in front of a rotary snowplow, 1928.   AHFAM (Alaska RR Collection)

Through the years, a wide variety of equipment has been used to clear the snow along the track. These large rotary snowplows have proven very effective for removing deep snow.

AHFAM (Alaska RR Collection)

These plows show the effects that snow and cold temperatures can have on equipment.

AHFAM (Alaska RR Collection)

Snowslides are frequent in the area around Turnagain Arm due to the steep terrain above the right-of-way. This slide occurred in 1951 at Mile 69.9 near Girdwood. AHFAM (Alaska RR Collection)

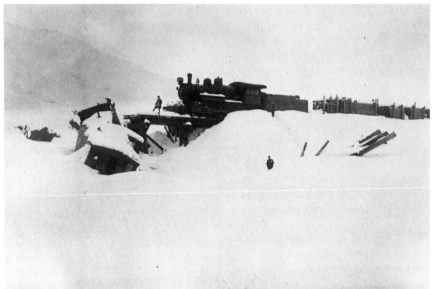

Mile 49.3, April 19, 1921.
AHL (Alaska RR Collection)

The Kenai Area receives very large snowfalls. In April 1921, a slide took out part of this trestle at Mile 49.
Top: AHL (Alaska RR Collection)
Bottom: UAA

Crewmen frantically dig for two men who were trapped in their train for 10 hours. The train was buried by a snowslide near Curry. No date.
AHFAM (Alaska RR Collection)

A freight train almost completely buried by a snowslide, near Curry, 1940s.
AHFAM (Alaska RR Collection)

Ice conditions in December 1946 at Mile 90.5. Similar conditions between miles 76 and 90.5 delayed trains for three days. The ice condition results from light snowfall coupled with extremely low temperatures. Wider cuts and better ditching helped eliminate this problem.
AHFAM (Alaska RR Collection)

In February 1946 a snowslide buried the track at Mile 71.8. The slide was dynamited and the snow then pushed away by bull-dozers. AHFAM (Alaska RR Collection)

An early Russell snowplow is pushed by two engines at Curry.
AHFAM (Alaska RR Collection)

WRECKS, FIRES, FLOODS

Derailment at Mile 13.4, May 4, 1948.

Derailment at Mile 174.5, near Houston, Aug. 9, 1971.

Derailment in the Fairbanks area, Dec. 28, 1949.

Snowslide at Mile 78, Jan. 5, 1920. Col. and Mrs. Frederick Mears were on board the train, but no one was injured.

AHFAM (Alaska RR Collection)

Wreck at Mile 91, January 1923.

AHFAM (Alaska RR Collection)

Snow is another enormous problem for the train crews. A constant vigil must be maintained for snowslides, especially in the Turnagain Arm area. This train ran into a snowslide at Bird Point in January 1980. No one was injured.

Photo by John Bowen, Alaska RR

Five empty boxcars were blown off the Bear Creek bridge, between Portage and Whittier, in February 1946. The deck also blew off the bridge.

Col. Mears and F.A. Hansen, construction engineer, inspecting wreck at Mile 49, April 12, 1921.

Tank-car derailment at Mile 355, July 29, 1949.   AHFAM (Alaska RR Collection)

It is very difficult to fight fire in the Alaskan interior's sub-zero temperatures as shown by this view of the backshop at the Fairbanks yards, March 3, 1950.   AHFAM (Alaska RR Collection)

Much damage was done to the coach shed and machine shop at the Anchorage yards fire in January 1951.

AHFAM (Alaska RR Collection)

The Healy roundhouse burned down on May 10, 1952, destroying some locomotives, AHFAM (Alaska RR Collection)

The Fairbanks yards under water during the disastrous August 1967 flood.
AHFAM (Alaska RR Collection)

Flooding has always been a threat to the railroad along the Tanana and Chena rivers. This photo was taken at Nenana in May 1948.
AHFAM (Alaska RR Collection)

THE 1964 EARTHQUAKE

On March 27, 1964, the Good Friday Earthquake dealt a devastating blow to the Alaska Railroad. The earthquake, the greatest ever recorded in North America, caused some $27 million worth of damage to Alaska's lifeline.

Damage was greatest between Seward and Anchorage. To the north, damage was less severe, but bridges were damaged as far away as Hurricane Gulch, 170 miles north of Anchorage.

The statistics staggered the imagination: three miles of main line carried away by landslides and tidal waves; eight miles of yard and dock tracks des-troyed; 560 wooden trestles destroyed or damaged. In addition, dozens of miles of main line track were exposed to tidal erosion, and, due to severe subsidence, subgrade on more than 50 miles of track was determined unsafe.

At Seward, the earthquake destroyed the deep-water marginal docks and transit sheds in addition to yard and dock tracks, more than 100 pieces of rolling stock, two large dockside gantry cranes and six large straddle buggies.

Whittier, the railroad's other southern port, suf-fered the loss of the car-barge slip, part of the depot

The swaying ground bent this stretch of track near Portage.

U.S. Army Corps of Engineers

and part of the wharf. At Anchorage, damage was considerable at the terminal yard and headquarter facilities and several buildings had to be razed.

The earthquake was a tremendous setback for the railroad, and the damage was compounded by the date of its occurrence—the roadbed was still frozen, complicating repairs. Yet the railroad responded quickly, and after a few days of intense damage inspection, officials decided first to make repairs north of Anchorage so that coal shipments could be resumed to military base power plants. Coal shipments began on April 6. Two weeks later the first train out of Whittier reached Anchorage with 125 freight cars. It took until September 13 to run the first freight from Seward north.

The railroad workers discovered that damage appeared in many forms. One of the main problems was the total subsidence of a part of the Kenai Peninsula that necessitated a major upbuilding of the railroad grade. Fortunately, the railroad's two tunnels to Whittier escaped harm, but it took many months to complete other repairs. The task was hindered by difficulty in obtaining equipment, as it was much in demand over many portions of the railroad, and major repairs, as usual, could be made only during the warmer months. Repairs were not completed until 1966.

The earthquake had been an event that probably heightened Alaskans' appreciation of the railroad, but it was an experience that no one was eager to go through again.

The port of Whittier also was hard hit. Top: Only one tower of the car-barge slip remained upright, and then only partially so. Bottom: Burning oil tanks. AHFAM (Alaska RR Collection)

The severe earthquake of March 27, 1964, devastated portions of the railroad from Seward to Anchorage. Shown here is the damage to Seward's railroad yards and docks after the area had been subjected to the earthquake, a tidal wave and fire.

More destruction in Seward.   U.S. Army Corps of Engineers

The Portage terminal was severely damaged.   AHFAM (Alaska RR Collection)

WORLD WAR II

Even before the attack on Pearl Harbor, the Alaska Railroad was intimately involved in building Alaska's defenses. With the establishment of military bases in Anchorage and Fairbanks in 1940 and 1941, the railroad experienced a dramatic increase in its haulage. At the same time, the railroad found it increasingly difficult to obtain labor due to increased military activity in Alaska and the Lower 48.

The increase in traffic and the inconvenience of shuffling staff members from the terminal site to the federal building prompted the railroad to begin construction of a three-story depot and general office building in Anchorage. It was completed in 1942 and is still in use today. To alleviate a bottleneck in traffic on the Kenai Peninsula, the railroad in 1941 also began construction, at a cost of $5.3 million, of that spur to the Passage Canal known as the Whittier Cutoff.

When the United States entered the war, the railroad became even more closely involved with Alaska's defense. Alaska was put under control of the Army, while the railroad was watched by civilian guards placed at strategic points along its route. A bypass was built around the famous "loop" to speed the flow of goods and as a precaution against enemy air attacks. A blackout rule, put in force throughout the state, made wintertime train operations hazardous.

The war also caused the railroad to undergo a labor shortage as many of its employees joined the military or left for higher-paying jobs. This problem was compounded by a critical shortage of locomotives and freight and passenger cars. Finally, the Alaska Defense Command loaned some soldiers to keep the trains operating and additional rolling stock was brought in, some of it from the defunct Copper River and Northwestern Railroad.

Troop train coming into Anchorage during the war.   AHFAM

Troops of the 4th Infantry Regiment arrive in Anchorage on June 27, 1940, from Seward. They were the vanguard of thousands of troops to be stationed in Alaska during the World War II years. Alaskan Air Command

But these measures were not enough. By early spring 1943, it was obvious that something had to be done to keep the railroad operating in a safe and efficient manner. Help was on its way in the form of the 714th Railway Operating Battalion, a part of the U.S. Army Transportation Corps.

Activated at Camp Claiborne, La., in March 1942, the battalion was made up for the most part of experienced railroad men from the Chicago, St. Paul, Minneapolis and Omaha Railroad. It was ordered to travel to Fort Lewis, Wash., to pick up additional track-maintenance personnel, and it headed for Alaska with a total of 23 commissioned officers, two warrant officers, and 1,092 enlisted men.

The battalion landed at Seward on April 3, 1943, and immediately went to work to augment the rail-road's slim civilian workforce. Maintenance was at a low ebb, and, due to the manpower shortage, there was a tremendous backlog of material piled up at Seward.

The opening of the port of Whittier later in 1943 alleviated some of this backlog, and other aid also came in 1943 with the arrival of six new locomotives, built by Baldwin for use overseas and numbered 551 to 556, similar to the 500-class locomotives already in service on the Alaska Railroad. Still, the men of the 714th had all they could contend with trying to run the railroad in tough winter conditions with barely enough personnel to do the job.

The Army also supplied soldiers for another vital railroad activity. A coal shortage developed in Alaska during the war due to the military's demands for fuel and the lack of miners to supply it. Thus the Army sent soldiers to keep the railroad's Eska coal mine open between 1942 and 1945.

During the war, Army personnel in Alaska sometimes stayed at the McKinley Park Hotel, which had been taken over by the Army as a recreation camp. The railroad operated a Brill car and trailer to the hotel from Anchorage, making a round trip each week.

In the aftermath of the expulsion of the Japanese from Alaska in 1943, the military relaxed a little, and its presence began to diminish in the territory. The War Manpower Commission recruited more civilian workers for the railroad in early 1945, and the 714th was released in May of that year.

With the end of the war, the railroad returned to its prewar schedule. The war had been an exhausting trial for the railroad, and considerable capital was needed to bring it back to safe operating conditions. But, with its return to a civilian role, the railroad knew it had contributed in its own way to the war effort.

Housing for the 714th Engineer Railway Operating Battalion, Anchorage, May 1943. The housing area was called the "Snake Ranch" by some. AHFAM (U.S. Army Collection)

The transshipping port of Nenana, on the Tanana River, was a busy place during the war. The railroad was the major transporter of material to interior Alaska and to the Alaska Highway.

U.S. Army (Top: SC #333854)
(Bottom: SC #207112)

Soldiers leaving the Mount McKinley station after a rest at the McKinley Park Hotel. The hotel was taken over by the Army during the war.   U.S. Army Military History Institute

An Army MT boat, one of the shallow-draft tugs used in rafting operations on the Tanana River, brought to Nenana by flatcar in 1944.   U.S. Army (SC #207110)

The Army's operations spanned more than 400 miles of railroad, and the PX had to be located where the Army was operating. This mobile PX moved up and down the line, dispensing personal items such as toilet articles, cigarettes, candy and magazines. The motor coach and trailer, sometimes called the "galloping goose" or "gray goose," occasionally served as an ambulance. U.S. Army (SC #337850)

Troop sleepers of the Alaska Railroad, 1947. The same cars were used during the war. AHFAM

WHITTIER

When the Alaska Railroad first was constructed, it reached only one deep-water port, at Seward, on the south shore of the Kenai Peninsula. With the looming of World War II, however, the U.S. military decided that the railroad should be extended to a second port in order to ensure a steady flow of personnel and equipment to the military installations that were being built at Anchorage and in Alaska's interior.

Thus the Whittier Cutoff was constructed by the U.S. Army, a 12.4-mile branch line that runs from the main line on the Kenai Peninsula, through the mountains on the peninsula's east side, to the port of Whittier, on the Passage Canal of Prince William Sound. The cutoff, which includes tunnels of 13,090 feet and 4,910 feet, shortened the distance from tidewater to Anchorage by 51.5 miles. In addition to providing a second deep-water port, the cutoff was built at a very low elevation and thus avoided some of the weather problems that plagued the higher-elevation main line route to Seward, the other deep-water port on the Kenai.

Packers had used the cutoff route long before anyone had thought of building a railroad there. When the railroad first was under construction earlier in the century, the cutoff route had been investigated and a survey had been made, but World War I and construction problems had put an end to the idea.

With the defense buildup in Alaska from 1940 on, the Whittier Cutoff route again came to light. A transportation bottleneck existed on the Kenai Peninsula, especially at the port of Seward, and military planners were concerned that this bottleneck would hinder shipments to the two air bases under construction at Anchorage and Fairbanks. Thus a feeder branch line was planned to the port of Whittier, where oceangoing vessels could unload supplies from the Lower 48, and ship them by rail to Alaska's interior. The port also offered a more protected harbor than Seward from possible enemy attack.

The final route for the 12-mile spur was determined in the spring of 1941, and the construction contract went to the West Construction Co. of Boston, Mass. The spur would connect with the main line at Portage (Milepost 64.2), and it would require the Army to build two tunnels as well as new dock facilities at Whittier.

The construction took longer than planned due to severe fall and winter weather, some poor planning, and wartime shortages of material and labor. The two tunnels were the most difficult part of the project. Work began on the tunnels with the facing off of surface material from the portal areas in August 1941. Over a year later, and after the excavation of over 98,000 cubic yards of solid rock, Maj. Gen. Simon B. Buckner, commander of the Alaska Defense Command, touched off the final blast during the holing-through ceremonies on Nov. 20, 1942. Due to shortages of rail, tracklaying was not started until late December of that year.

The first passenger train went through the tunnels on March 10, 1943, when an official party took Brill Car #114 and a trailer to Whittier for a meeting with the contractor. The Whittier Cutoff was placed in regular operation on June 1, 1943, two years after construction began, although construction of the Whittier terminal and dock facilities, which had begun in July 1942, had not yet been completed.

The Army routed all of its traffic through the new port and the cutoff for the remainder of the war, while commercial vessels continued to use the port of Seward. It was estimated that the cutoff permitted the railroad to handle approximately 75 percent more tonnage than the tonnage handled by the Seward port alone.

Whittier also was the destination of the first diesel engines on the Alaska Railroad. The run was made on June 15, 1944, by engines #1000 and #1001, standard 1,000-horsepower road switching locomotives built by the American Locomotive Co. The two could be coupled together and operated from a single cab.

In December 1945, following the end of the war, the Alaska Railroad took over operation of the Whittier dock facilities from the Army, but the Army briefly took back the facilities in 1946 and took them back permanently in 1949.

The Army constructed a major petroleum-hand-

Before setting off the blast to open the tunnel to Whittier, Maj. Gen. Simon B. Buckner, commander of the Alaska Defense Command, and party gather at the tunnel entrance. Nov. 20, 1942.

AHFAM (Alaska RR Collection)

Holing-through ceremonies on Nov. 20, 1942. Col. Otto F. Ohlson, left, shakes hands with Maj. Gen. S.B. Buckner.

AHFAM (Alaska RR Collection)

Climbing through debris after the blast. The explosion completed the tunnel, located on the Whittier Cutoff route.

AHFAM (Alaska RR Collection)

ling facility at Whitter to supply Alaska's military installations, and in 1952, it completed a large seven-story building at the port, naming it after General Buckner. This provided housing for 1,700 people, and it included most of the amenities of a small city—all under one roof. The miltary believed that, in view of Whittier's severe winters, one large building would be more comfortable and cost efficient than many scattered small buildings. A second structure, the massive, 14-story Hodge Building, was constructed at Whittier in the mid-1950s to house additional personnel.

In addition to severe winters, Whittier also has had its share of other disasters. A fire in 1953 destroyed the entire cargo-handling facility, and temporary prefabricated docks were brought up from the south and used until new docks were constructed in 1957. The 1964 earthquake also did considerable damage to the port facilities.

In the fall of 1960, the Army finally deactivated the port of Whittier and turned over operations to the Alaska Railroad. Whittier is now the railroad's major port. It handles rail-barge shipments from the Lower 48 and from Canada, as well as traffic to and from Valdez on the Alaska Marine Highway ferry service.

South portal, Whittier Tunnel, showing drifted snow, April 1943.   AHFAM (Alaska RR Collection)

View of the upper end of Whittier, showing the U.S. Army barracks. September 1943. AHFAM (Alaska RR Collection)

General view of Whittier during the war years.   AHFAM (Alaska RR Collection)

Dock facilities at Whittier, June 1943. With the completion of the cutoff in late 1942, Whittier provided a much shorter and safer route to Anchorage for the thousands of tons of cargo that were pouring into Alaska during the war.

AHFAM (Alaska RR Collection)

General view of Whittier area, looking northeast, June 1943. The railroad yards are on the left and the dock area is in the center background.

AHFAM (Alaska RR Collection)

Diesel engine #1001 at Whittier. It was one of the first four diesels that were placed in service in June 1944. AHFAM (Alaska RR Collection)

Whittier, just after the war.

AHFAM (Alaska RR Collection)

The Whittier railroad station, May 1944.
U.S. Army (SC #571430)

Whittier in 1950.
AHFAM (Alaska RR Collection)

Whittier in 1950.
AHFAM (Alaska RR Collection)

Whittier barge slip, March 1964. Soon afterwards, it was destroyed in the Good Friday Earthquake.

AHFAM (Alaska RR Collection)

The new barge slip, built after the 1964 earthquake.

AHFAM (Alaska RR Collection)

Ferry dock at Whittier.

AHFAM (Alaska RR Collection)

This magnificent 14-story building was built in the 1950s to provide additional housing. It is still in use.

The Buckner Building was built in 1952 by the U.S. Army for housing and service functions. It is not in use at present.

Other buildings in Whittier built in the post-war years are abandoned or rarely used.

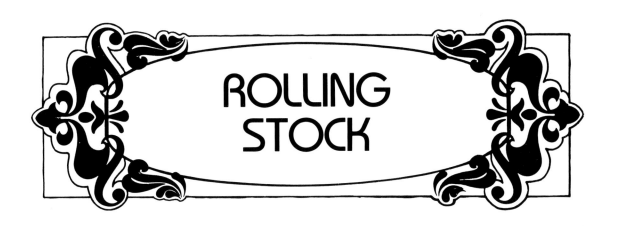

ROLLING STOCK

Baldwin 4-8-2 #801. The locomotive was built in 1932 and was badly damaged in 1942 when it ran into a snowslide between Potter and Indian. It was rebuilt, but had another wreck in 1951.   AHFAM (Alaska RR Collection)

Lima 2-8-0 locomotive, purchased from the U.S. Army in 1942. After being put into service, the "500" series was renumbered with 400-series designations.

AHFAM (Alaska RR Collection)

Dinkey engine #22, obtained by the A.E.C. from the Isthmus Canal Commission in 1917. A narrow-gauge saddle-tanker, it was used by various coal mining operations in the Matanuska Valley.
AHFAM (Alaska RR Collection)

A narrow-gauge motor car used between Nenana and Fairbanks in 1920. It hauled passengers between the two points when no regular service was scheduled.
AHFAM (Alaska RR Collection)

Nenana, *a Brill railbus, could carry 24 passengers and was used on short runs and during periods of light traffic.*
AHFAM (Alaska RR Collection)

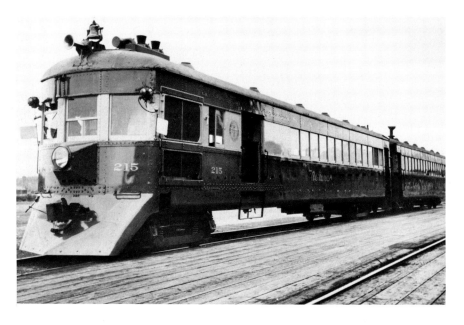

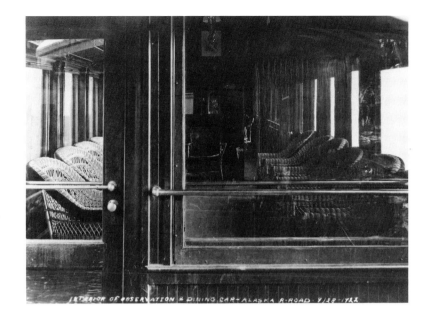

Interior of observation/ dining car, 1922.
AHL (Alaska RR Collection)

Interior of a coach car.
AHFAM (Alaska RR Collection)

The passenger cars Nenana *and* Chugach, *in the 1930s.*
AHFAM (Alaska RR Collection)

Wooden caboose, built in 1916.
AHFAM (Alaska RR Collection)

The Anchorage-Chickaloon mixed train at Matanuska Junction, April 1919.
AHFAM (Alaska RR Collection)

A 1940 Pontiac railmobile used by railroad officials for inspection trips.
AHFAM (Alaska RR Collection)

Spreader at work, 1920s.
AHL (Alaska RR Collection)

A Jordan Spreader at Mile 219, July 1948.
AHFAM (Alaska RR Collection)

A "Snow-Go," used for cleaning snow from the tracks, 1948.
AHFAM (Alaska RR Collection)

The observation car
Seward, *1948.*
    AHFAM (Alaska RR Collection)

Troop sleeper, used during World War II.
    AHFAM (Alaska RR Collection)

Several of the World War II troop sleepers are now on display at the Alaska Transportation Museum in Palmer.

Diesel locomotive #1050, in 1946. The locomotive, also identified as G.E. #8040, was formerly used by the U.S. Army. It was acquired by the railroad after World War II and used into the mid-1960s. AHFAM (Alaska RR Collection)

A modern caboose in Bicentennial markings.

Diesel locomotive #1508.

AHFAM (Alaska RR Collection)

Diesel locomotive #1050, October 1947.

FREIGHT EQUIPMENT

The freight cars of this Railroad are marked "A. R. R." and numbered and classified as follows:

KIND OF CARS		NUMBERS	DIMENSIONS												CAPACITY		No.
			Inside			Outside					Doors						
								Height from Rail			Side		End				
M. B. C. Designation	CLASS		Length	Width	Height	Length	Width at Eaves or Platform	To Eaves	To Top of Platform or Runn'g Board	To over all	Width	Height	Width	Height	Cubic Feet Level Full	Pounds or Gallons	
			ft. in.	ft. in.	ft. in.	ft. in.	ft. in.	ft. in.	ft. in.	ft. in.	ft. in.	ft. in.	ft. in.	ft. in.			
XM	Box	801— 850	36 0	8 6	8 5	36 11½	9 7½	12 5⅛	13 1¼	13 7⅝	6 0	7 6½	2 0	3 0	2448	60000	37
XM	Box	851— 853	39 0	8 6	8 0	40 0	9 7½	12 5	13 1¼	13 7⅝	6 0	7 6½			2652	80000	3
XI	Hot	902— 922	37 0	7 9	7 5	38 0		11 9	12 5	13 1	5 0	7 2			2126	80000	21
XA	Auto	1101—1104	39 0	8 6	8 0	40 0	9 7½	12 5	13 1¼	13 7⅝	10 0	8 0	8 2	8 0		80000	4
FM	Flat	701— 756				41 0	8 9½		3 7							80000	38
FM	Flat	2001—2475				40 0	9 3		3 10							80000	335
CM	Coal	4001—4158	37 3	8 0	4 0	40 0	9 3		7 10						1291	80000	152
SM	Stock	1301—1306	40 0	7 8¼	8 3	41 0	9 0	12 1¾	12 11	13 10¾	5 0	8 0			2550	80000	6
GD	Gondola	1201—1213	36 10	8 3¼	5 4	41 0	9 3¾		3 7	9 7	4 8	5 3			1326	80000	12
GA	Gondola	5001—5040	30 0	8 9	6 7	30 5	10 1		4 0	10 7					1536	100000	40
RM	Refrigerator	1501—1506	28 9	8 4	7 6	36 11½	9 7½	12 5¼	12 11	13 6¼	4 0	5 9⅞	†1 6⅛	†1 9¾	1797	60000	6
MWB	Ballast	1401—1446	40 0	8 8	3 0	41 6	9 10		4 6½	8 4½	4 7	2 8⅝	8 7	3 0	1040	100000	46
MWB	Ballast	1601—1631	33 0	8 8	3 11	36 10	9 2		4 3½	9 6	4 2	2 9	8 8	3 11	1145	80000	31
MWD	Dump	501— 536	19 0	9 0	1 10½	22 5	9 11		5 9½	7 10					324	40000	38
MWD	Dump	551— 589	19 0	9 0	1 10½	21 0	10 0		6 6½	7 4					324	40000	37
MWD	Dump	1— 30	25 0	9 0	2 4½	27 6	9 11		5 10	8 10					513	80000	29
MWD	Dump	402— 409	28 6¾	9 5¼	2 8½	35 2½	10 6			7 10					675	100000	8
MWD	Dump	401	34 6¾	9 5¼	2 8½	41 2½	10 6			7 10					810	100000	1
																Total	844

† Side door at end for Oil Heaters.

PASSENGER EQUIPMENT

M.C.B Designation	KIND	Series of Numbers	Seating Cap'c'ty	Length of Car		No.
				ft.	in.	
PB	Coach—Steel	11—12	68	69	0	2
PB	Coach—Steel	14—16	75	72	0	3
PB	Coach—Steel	17—18	84	80	0	2
PB	Coach	1&3-4&6-9	56	58	6	7
MB	Mail & Baggage—Steel	61—64		65	0	4
MB	Mail & Baggage	51—54		36	11½	4
PV	Business Car	B-1	14	58	6	1
PS	Sleeper	Anchorage Chatanika	20	64	2	2
PC	Parlor Car	Tanana	25	64	2	1
PO	Observation	Yukon	40	81	8½	1

M.C.B. Designation	KIND	Series of Numbers	Seating Cap'c'ty	Length		No.
				ft.	in.	
PO	Observation	Denali	40	81	3	1
PO	Observation	Kenai	36	69	3	1
PO	Observation	Nenana	20	53	4	1
CS	Comb. Smoking & Baggage	81—82	32	64	2	2
DA	Diner	71	28	64	2	1
ED	Brill-Gas, Electric	114	26	60	3	1
PB	Brill-Trailer	303	60	50	10	1
EG	Brill Gas Car	107	48	56	6	1
EG	McKeen Gas Car	108	40			1

Total 37

LOCOMOTIVES

Class.	TYPE	Tractive Power	No.
200	Mogul 2-6-0	23980	9
600	Mogul 2-6-0	24690	7
700	Mikado 2-8-2	42600	3
31	Mikado 2-8-2		1
1-5-6	Saddle Tank	15350	3
		Total	23

MISCELLANEOUS EQUIPMENT

KIND	Series of Numbers	No.	KIND	Series of Numbers	No.	KIND	Series of Numbers	No.
Steam Shovels	3-6-7&9	4	Russell Snow Plows	1-2	2	Tool Cars	251-2348	2
Ditchers	101-102	2	Tank Cars	1 to 9	9	Spreaders	1 to 3	3
Crane Ditcher	103	1	Outfit Cars	02x to 036x	33	Lidgerwoods	1-2	2
Track Driver	6	1	Wreck. Tool Car	001	1	Caboose Cars	1001 to 1021	16
Loco. Cranes	1 to 7	7	Wreck. Outfit Car	002	1	Motor Cars	102, 104, 106, 109-116	9
Rotary Snow Plows	1 to 3	3	Wreck. Truck Car	004	1	Wrecking Crane	55	1

Total 98

Equipment roster, 1931. AHFAM (Alaska RR Collection)

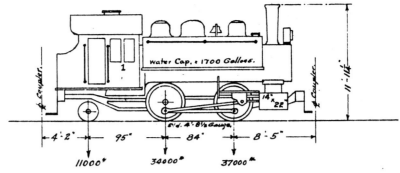

Water Cap. : 1700 Gallons.

1

14"×22"

Std. 4' 8½" Gauge.

4'-2"   95"   84"   8'-5"

11000#   34000#   37000#

A.R.R. - CLASS A1 - SADDLE TANK LOCOMOTIVE.

- SPECIFICATIONS -

Purchased from	- American Locomotive Company.
New Equipment.	
Placed in Service	- Anchorage 1916.
Estimated Life	- 20 Years.
Type	- Saddle Tank, 0-4-2.
Builder	- American Locomotive Company - Rogers Works.
Cylinders	- 14"×22"
Dia. of Drivers	- 44"
Wt. on Drivers	- 71000 #
Total Wt. Engine	- 82000 #
Tractive Power	- 13350 #
Hauling Capacity	- 2320 Tons on Level Track.
Valve Gear	- Link Valve Gear with Sliding Valve.
Driving Wheel Base	= 7'-0"
Total Eng. Wheel Base	= 14'-11"
Driving Journals	: 7"×8"
Maximum Height	= 11'-11¼"
Maximum Width	: 8'-8"
No Tender - Saddle Tank. - Capacity : 1700 Gallons.	
Couplers	- M.C.B. "Tower" Pocket.

Train Length	- 27'-6"
Pilot	- None.
Fuel	- Bituminous.

Engine is equipped with Automatic Air Brakes, Steel Cab, Steel Tired Truck Wheels, W.I. Frames, Hand Sander for Forward and Reverse and other usual Accessories, Oil Headlight.

BOILER -	
Working Pressure	- 165 Lbs.
Heating Surface	- 660 Sq.Ft. Approx.
Length	- 12'-2 5/16"
Diameter	- 43"
Number of Tubes	- 106
Length of Tubes	- 11'-8"
Dia. of Tubes	- 2"

#1 + 5

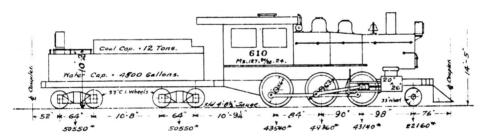

Coal Cap. - 12 Tons.

610

M2.127.26/60.24.

Water Cap. - 4500 Gallons.

33" C.I. Wheels

Std. 4'-8½" Gauge.

20"×26"

33" Wheel

14'-5"

52"   64"   10'-8"   64"   10'-9½"   84"   90"   98"   76"

50550#   50550#   43540#   44360#   43140#   22160#

A.R.R. - CLASS M2 - MOGUL TYPE LOCOMOTIVE.

- SPECIFICATIONS -

Panama Canal Equipment - (Originally constructed 5 Ft. Gauge. Wheels have been Pressed in to Standard 4'-8½" Gauge.)
Second Hand.

Placed in Service	- Anchorage 1919
Estimated Life	- 15 Years.
Builder	- American Locomotive Company - Brooks Works.
Type	- Mogul - 2-6-0.
Cylinders	- 20"×26" - 20½"×27" on 601
Dia. of Drivers	- 63" - 54" on 601
Wt. on Drivers	- 136040 #
Total Wt. Engine	- 158200 #
Total Wt. Engine & Tender	- 259300 #
Tractive Power	- 24690# at 10 miles per Hour.
Hauling Capacity	- 3447 Tons on Level Track.
Valve Gear	- Stephenson Link, with Richardson Balanced Slide Valve.
Driving Wheel Base	- 14'-6"
Total Engine Wheel Base	- 22'-8"
Driving Journals	- 9"×11"
Maximum Height	- 14'-5"
Maximum Width	- 9'-10"
8 Wheel Tender, Square-End Tank.	
Coal Capacity	- 12 Tons.
Water Capacity	- 4500 Gallons.
Journals	- 5"×9"
Under-frame.	- Steel.

Couplers	- M.C.B. "Tower" Pocket.
Train Length (Engine & Tender)	- 65'-5"

Originally no Pilot on Engine - Equipped with Steel Pilot at Anchorage.
Fuel — Bituminous Coal.
Engine is equipped with Automatic & Straight Air Brakes, Steel Cab, Steel Tired Truck Wheels, W.I. Frames, Leach pneumatic Sander for Forward & Reverse and other usual accessories, Pyle National Electric Headlight, Engine has double Air-pipe line with 4-Way Engineer's Valve and Standard Hose Connections for use with Air-dump Cars.
Steam Dome is Tapped with 3" Pipe for use with the Lingerwood Unloader.

BOILER	
Working Pressure	- 180 Lbs. - 190 # on 620
Heating Surface	- 2203 Sq.Ft.
Length	- 25'-11½"
Diameter	- 6'-1¾"
Number of Tubes	- 316
Length of Tubes	- 12'-3 3/16"
Dia. of Tubes	- 2"
Grate Area	- 31 sq.ft.

Total Number = 6 - 605 - 606 - 610 - 614 - 618 - 620.
ENG 601 CHANGED DRIVERS TO 54" DIA INSIDE

-131-

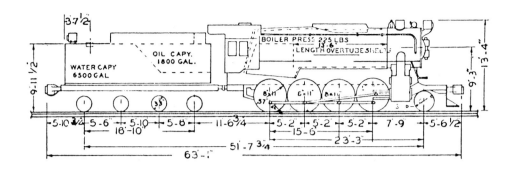

BUILT BY BALDWIN LOCO. WORKS	LENGTH OF FIREBOX INSIDE 84 1/8"
DATE BUILT 1943	WIDTH OF FIREBOX INSIDE 70 1/4"
TYPE CONSOLIDATION	GRATE AREA 41.04 SQ FT.
WEIGHT ON DRIVERS W.O. 141,000 LBS.	SIZE OF BOILER TUBES 2"-13'-6"
WEIGHT ON FRONT TRUCK W.O. 21,500 LBS.	NUMBER OF TUBES 150
WEIGHT ON BACK TRUCK W.O. NONE	SIZE OF SUPERHEATER FLUES 5 3/8"-13'-6"
TOTAL WEIGHT OF ENGINE W.O. 162,500 LBS.	NUMBER OF SUPERHEATER FLUES 30
TOTAL WEIGHT OF TENDER LOADED 126,500 LBS.	TOTAL HEATING SURFACE 1773 SQ FT.
TOTAL WEIGHT OF ENG. & TEN. LOADED 189,000 LBS.	SUPERHEATER 480 SQ FT. ELESCO TYPE A
CYLINDERS 19"x26"	VALVE GEAR WALSCHAERT
DIA. OF DRIVERS 57"	POWER REVERSE GEAR - BALDWIN
TRACTIVE POWER (85% BOILER PRESS.) 31,500 LBS.	AIR PUMP WESTINGHOUSE
FACTOR OF ADHESION 4.4	8 1/2 CROSS COMPOUND
MAXIMUM WIDTH OVERALL 8'-11 1/2"	BRAKE SCHEDULE 6-ET
FUEL DIESEL OIL	557 OIL BURNER
BRICKARCH AMERICAN SECURITY	TENDER CAPY. 1800 GAL. OIL
BOILER PRESS. 225 LBS	HEIGHT CENTER OF GRAVITY ENGINE 67"
	HEIGHT CENTER OF GRAVITY TENDER 80 1/2"

NO. 701, 702, 703
MIKADO TYPE

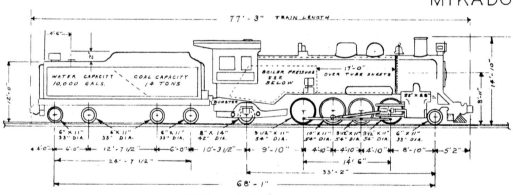

	NOS. 701-702	NO. 703		
BUILT BY - BALDWIN LOCO. WKS.			LENGTH OF FIREBOX INSIDE	115 1/8"
DATE BUILT	1927	1928	WIDTH OF FIREBOX INSIDE	72 1/4"
PURCHASED FROM - B.L.WORKS	NEW	NEW	GRATE AREA	57.7 SQ. FT.
PLACED IN SERVICE	1927	1928	SIZE OF BOILER TUBES	2"X 17'-0"
TOTAL WT. OF ENG. & TENDER	441680	441400	SIZE OF SUPERHEATER FLUES	5 3/8" X 17'-0"
TOTAL WT. OF ENG.	244400	244120	NO. OF SUPERHEATER FLUES	32
TOTAL WT. OF TENDER	197280	197280	TOTAL HEATING SURFACE	2718 SQ. FT.
WT. ON DRIVERS	172360	175680	SUPERHEATER	621 SQ. FT.
WT. ON FRONT TRUCK	23130	23130	VALVE GEAR	BAKER
WT. ON BACK TRUCK	45310	45310	POWER REVERSE GEAR	BALDWIN
CYLINDERS	22"X 28"	22"X 28"	ARCH TUBES	4
TRACT. POWER-LBS.(85% B.P.)	42600	44800	FACTOR OF ADHESION	5.44
BOILER PRESSURE LBS.	200	210	MAXIMUM WIDTH OVERALL	10'-5"
NUMBER OF BOILER TUBES	192	193		

SUPERHEATER	SCHMIDT TYPE "A"
AIR PUMP	ONE 8 1/2" CROSS COMPOUND
STOKER	SIMPLEX TYPE "B-K"
LOW WATER ALARM	BARCO TYPE "F-3A"
BRICK ARCH	AMERICAN SECURITY

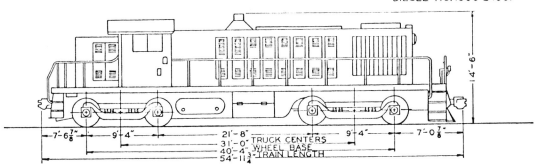

Dimensions on drawing: 14'-6" (height); 7'-6⅞" | 9'-4" | 21'-8" TRUCK CENTERS | 9'-4" | 7'-0⅞"; 31'-0" WHEEL BASE; 40'-4" TRAIN LENGTH; 54'-11¾"

BUILT BY	AMERICAN LOCO. CO.	GEAR RATIO	16/75
DATE BUILT	1944	SUPPLIES TOTAL CAPY.	
PLACED IN SERVICE	1944	LUBRICATING OIL	80 GALS
PURCHASED FROM	AMERICAN LOCO. CO.	FUEL OIL	1600 GALS
WHEEL DIA.	40"	TOTAL	1680 GALS
JOURNALS	7"X14"	SAND	27 CU. FT.
MAX. GOVERNED SPEED	740 R.P.M.	MAX. SAFE SPEED	60 M.P.H.
IDLING SPEED	275 R.P.M.	MAX. TRACTIVE EFFORT W/ ½ VARIABLE SUPPLIES	
CYLINDERS	6-CYL.	AT 25% ADHESION	61,250#
BORE	12½"	MIN. CURVE RADIUS	100 FT.
STROKE	13"	MAX. OVERALL DIMENSIONS:	
WT. IN WORKING ORDER	245,000# W/ALL SUPPLIES	HEIGHT	14'-6"
WT. ON DRIVERS	245,000#	WIDTH	10'-4"
AIRBRAKE SCHEDULE	EL-14	TRAIN LENGTH	54'-11¾"
BRAKE CYLINDERS	8 (4-9"X8" EACH TRUCK)	ENG. COOLING WATER	240 GALS
AIR COMPRESSOR	WEST. 3 C.D.		

1000 H.P. ALCO MODEL 539
BOILER CAPY. & MODEL—1600 PER HR. {1000, DK 74/4530
BOILER WATER CAPY. 800 GALS {1001, CFK 4160/28

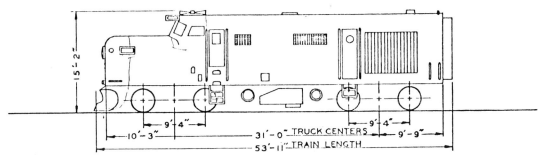

Dimensions on drawing: 15'-2" (height); 10'-3" | 9'-4" | 31'-0" TRUCK CENTERS | 9'-4" | 9'-9"; 53'-11" TRAIN LENGTH

BUILT BY	AMERICAN LOCOMOTIVE CO.	GEAR RATIO	16:75
DATE BUILT	1943	SUPPLIES TOTAL CAPY.	
PLACED IN SERVICE	1947	LUBRICATING OIL	80 GALS
PURCHASED FROM	WAR SURPLUS	FUEL OIL	1600 GALS
WHEEL DIA.	40"	TOTAL	1680 GALS
JOURNALS	TIMKEN R.B. 7"X14"	SAND	24 CU. FT.
MAX. GOVERNED SPEED	740 R.P.M.	MAX. SAFE SPEED	60 M.P.H.
IDLING SPEED	275 R.P.M.	MAX. TRACTIVE EFFORT W ½ VARIABLE SUPPLIES AT 30%	
CYLINDERS	6-CYL.	ADHESION	75,000#
BORE	12½"	MAX. CURVATURE DEGREE	16 DEG.
STROKE	13"	MAX. OVERALL DIMENSIONS:	
WT. IN WORKING ORDER	254,000# W/ALL SUPPLIES	HEIGHT	15'X2"
WT. ON DRIVERS	254,000#	WIDTH	10'-6"
AIRBRAKE SCHEDULE	14EL.	TRAIN LENGTH	53'-11"
BRAKE CYLINDERS	8 (4-9"X8" EACH TRUCK)	ENG. COOLING WATER	240 GALS
AIR COMPRESSOR	S-16	1000 H.P. MODEL 539 ENGINE	
REBUILT BY	I.R.C.E.M. CO.		

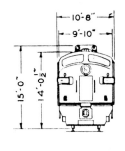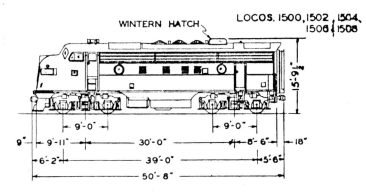

LOCOS. 1500, 1502, 1504, 1506 & 1508

WINTERN HATCH

BUILT BY	GENERAL MOTORS CORP, E.M.D.	
DATE BUILT	LOCOS. 1500,1502 & 1504 - DEC. 1952	
	LOCOS. 1506 1508 - DEC. 1953	
PLACED IN SERVICE	JAN. 1953 & JAN. 1954	
PURCHASED FROM	G.M.C. - E.M.D.	
WHEEL DIA.	40 INCHES	
JOURNALS	HYATT - 6½ x 12"	
MAX. GOVERNED SPEED	800 R.P.M.	
IDLING SPEED	275 R.P.M.	
CYLINDERS	16	
BORE	8½	
STROKE	10"	
W.T. IN WORKING ORDER	245,500 LBS. W/ALL SUPPLIES	
W.T. ON DRIVERS	245,500 LBS.	
AIRBRAKE SCHEDULE	6 BL	
BRAKE CYLINDERS	9" x 8"	
AIR COMPRESSOR	GARDNER-DENVER	
	LOCOS. 1500,1502 & 1504 , WXE-8035	
	LOCO. 1506 , WXE-8038	
	LOCO. 1508 , WXO-8015	
OVERNITE HEATER	VAPOR-CLARKSON -4915	

GEAR RATIO	62:15
SUPPLIES TOTAL CAP'Y.	
LUBRICATING OIL	200 GALS.
FUEL OIL LOCOS 1506 & 1508	1200 GALS.
ENG COOLING WATER	235 GALS.
SAND	16 CU.FT.
MAX. SAFE SPEED	65 M.P.H.
MAX. OVERALL DIMENSIONS	
HEIGHT	15'-9½"
WIDTH	10'-8"
TRAIN LENGTH	50'-8"
WHEEL BASE - TRUCK	9'-0"
MAX. CURVATURE DEGREE	23°
FUEL OIL 1500, 1502 & 1504	1500 GALS.
CENTER OF GRAVITY ABOVE RAIL	83"
MAX. TRACTIVE EFFORT W/½ VARIABLE SUPPLIES	
AT 25% ADHESION	59870 LBS.

MODEL F7-A LEAD UNIT- 1500 H.P.
1502 & 1508 EQUIPPED W/DYNAMIC BRAKES 1954
1506 " " " " 1956

Nos 1100 to 1107

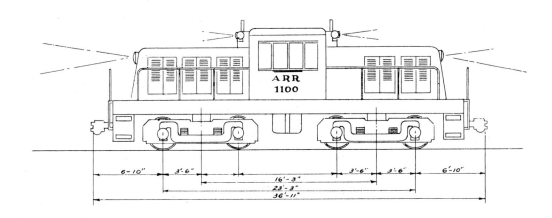

ARR 1100

BUILT BY R.K. PORTER CO.	DEC. 1942	
TYPE: PORTER CUMMINS DIESEL		
(2) 4-WHEEL SWIVEL TRUCKS		
PURCHASED FROM SURPLUS PROP. U.S. ARMY		
PLACED IN SERVICE	FEB. 1947	
WEIGHT	130,000 LBS.	
400 H.P.		
2 HIGH SPEED GENERATORS		
4 LOW SPEED MOTORS		
TRACTIVE FORCE AT 30% ADHESION	39,000 LBS.	
TRACTIVE FORCE CONTINOUS RATING		
	5,600 LBS. AT 10 M.P.H.	

WHEEL BASE - TRUCKS	7'-0"
TOTAL WHEEL BASE	23'-3"
LENGTH OVER BUMPERS	34'-0"
TRAIN LENGTH	36'-11"
HEIGHT	12'-0"
WIDTH	9'-6"

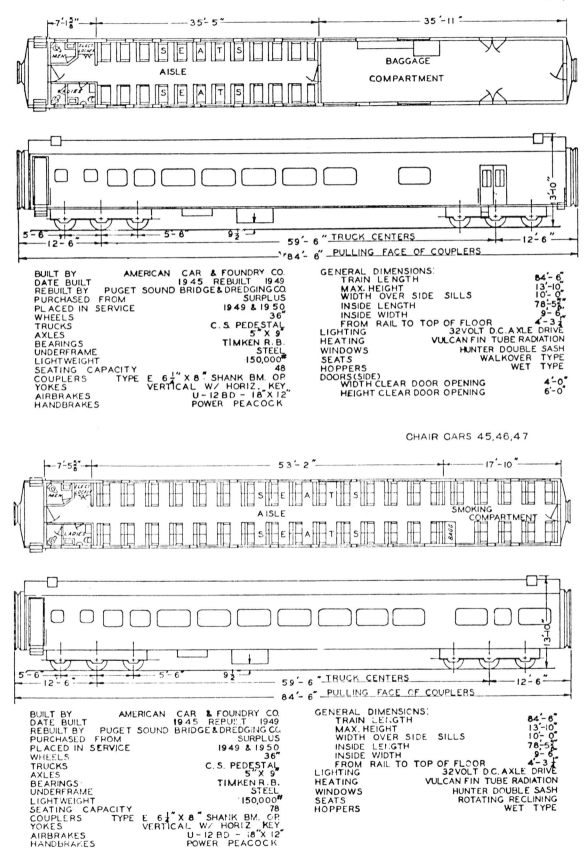

7'-1⅝"   35'-5"   35'-11"

SEATS

AISLE

BAGGAGE

COMPARTMENT

SEATS

3'-10"

5'-6"   5'-6"   9½"   59'-6" TRUCK CENTERS   12'-6"
12'-6"   84'-6" PULLING FACE OF COUPLERS

BUILT BY	AMERICAN CAR & FOUNDRY CO.
DATE BUILT	1945 REBUILT 1949
REBUILT BY	PUGET SOUND BRIDGE & DREDGING CO.
PURCHASED FROM	SURPLUS
PLACED IN SERVICE	1949 & 1950
WHEELS	36"
TRUCKS	C. S. PEDESTAL
AXLES	5" X 9"
BEARINGS	TIMKEN R.B.
UNDERFRAME	STEEL
LIGHTWEIGHT	150,000#
SEATING CAPACITY	48
COUPLERS	TYPE E 6½" X 8" SHANK BM. OP.
YOKES	VERTICAL W/ HORIZ. KEY
AIRBRAKES	U-12 BD - 18"X 12"
HANDBRAKES	POWER PEACOCK

GENERAL DIMENSIONS:	
TRAIN LENGTH	84'-6"
MAX. HEIGHT	13'-10"
WIDTH OVER SIDE SILLS	10'-0"
INSIDE LENGTH	78'-5½"
INSIDE WIDTH	9'-6"
FROM RAIL TO TOP OF FLOOR	4'-3¼"
LIGHTING	32 VOLT D.C. AXLE DRIVE
HEATING	VULCAN FIN TUBE RADIATION
WINDOWS	HUNTER DOUBLE SASH
SEATS	WALKOVER TYPE
HOPPERS	WET TYPE
DOORS (SIDE)	
WIDTH CLEAR DOOR OPENING	4'-0"
HEIGHT CLEAR DOOR OPENING	6'-0"

CHAIR CARS 45, 46, 47

7'-5⅝"   53'-2"   17'-10"

S E A T S

AISLE   SMOKING
COMPARTMENT

LADIES   S E A T S   BAGG

5'-6"   5'-6"   9½"   59'-6" TRUCK CENTERS   12'-6"
12'-6"   84'-6" PULLING FACE OF COUPLERS

13'-10"

BUILT BY	AMERICAN CAR & FOUNDRY CO.
DATE BUILT	1945 REBUILT 1949
REBUILT BY	PUGET SOUND BRIDGE & DREDGING CO.
PURCHASED FROM	SURPLUS
PLACED IN SERVICE	1949 & 1950
WHEELS	36"
TRUCKS	C. S. PEDESTAL
AXLES	5" X 9"
BEARINGS	TIMKEN R.B.
UNDERFRAME	STEEL
LIGHTWEIGHT	150,000#
SEATING CAPACITY	78
COUPLERS	TYPE E 6½" X 8" SHANK BM. OP.
YOKES	VERTICAL W/ HORIZ. KEY
AIRBRAKES	U-12 BD - 18"X 12"
HANDBRAKES	POWER PEACOCK

GENERAL DIMENSIONS:	
TRAIN LENGTH	84'-6"
MAX. HEIGHT	13'-10"
WIDTH OVER SIDE SILLS	10'-0"
INSIDE LENGTH	78'-5½"
INSIDE WIDTH	9'-6"
FROM RAIL TO TOP OF FLOOR	4'-3¼"
LIGHTING	32 VOLT D.C. AXLE DRIVE
HEATING	VULCAN FIN TUBE RADIATION
WINDOWS	HUNTER DOUBLE SASH
SEATS	ROTATING RECLINING
HOPPERS	WET TYPE

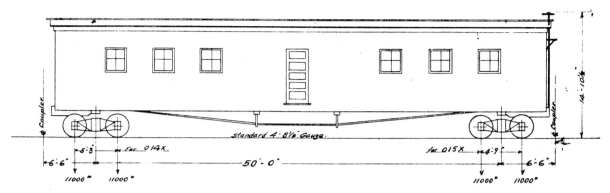

A.R.R. - "O" SERIES - OUTFIT DINING CARS "O-14-X & "O-15-X"
· SPECIFICATIONS ·

Built by A.E.C. at Anchorage
Placed in Service   - Anchorage 1918
Estimated Life   - 18 Years.
Lightweight   - 44000" Approx. Average.
Underframe   - Wood - 4 Sills.
          End Sills - 8"x10"x10'-0"
          Center Sills - 8"x10"x58'-10"
          Side Sills - 8"x10"x58'-10"
Decking   - 1½"x7" and Covered with 1" Flooring
Pocket for Couplers - 1"x4" Iron.
Couplers   - 5"x5" Shank - "Sharon" Top Lift.
Coupler Springs   - 6"x8"
Follower Plate
Draft Timbers   - 7"x7½"x4'-8¼"
Truss Rods   - Two 1½" - Turnbuckle 1¾"
Brake Beam   - Metal.
Bolster   - Wood - Car O-14-X
    "   - Structural Steel - Car O-15-X
Truck   - Arch Bar.
Center to Center-Trucks - 50'-0"

Wheel Base of Trucks - 5'-3" Car O-14-X
    "   "   "   - 4'-9" " O-15-X
Axles   - 4¼"x8 Journals.
Journal Boxes   - M.S.Cord Box & Cover.
Draft Gear   - Tandem Spring
Air Brakes   - Westinghouse.
GENERAL DIMENSIONS.
  Train Length   - 63'-0"
  Maximum Width - 10'-9"
  "   Height - 14'-10½"
  Inside Length   - 59'-0"
  "   Width   - 9'-3"
  "   Height   - 8'-8"
  Outside Length - 60'-0"
  Width at Eaves - 10'-9"
  Height Rail to Eaves - 13'-5½"
  " Rail - Running Board -14'-3½"
  End Doors   - 2'-6"x6'-6" High
  Side Doors   - 2'-6"x6'-6"

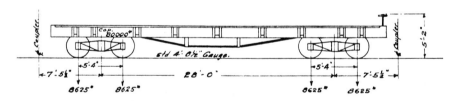

A.R.R. - 2000 SERIES - PANAMA FLAT CAR
· SPECIFICATIONS ·

Panama Canal Equipment - (Originally constructed 5 Ft. Gauge,
  Wheels have been Pressed in to Standard 4'-8½" Gauge)
Second Hand
Placed in Service   -Anchorage 1916-1917
Estimated Life   - 16 Years.
Lightweight   - 34500" Approx. Average.
Underframe   - Wood - 8 Sills.
          End Sill   - 8"x12"x9'-4"
          Intermediate Sill -5"x9"x39'-0"
          Center Sill -5"x9"x39'-0"
          Side Sill -5"x14"x39'-11"
Decking   - 3"x8"x9'-1"
Pocket for Couplers. -1"x4"x22"Iron -4"x5"x8½" Space Blocks.
Couplers   - 5"x7"x8½" "Tower" Undercut.
Coupler Springs   - 8"x8"
Follower Plates   - 1½"x8"x10" & 1½"x8"x7½"
Draft Timbers.   -4½"x5"x8'-0" Oak.
Truss Rods.   - Six 1½" - Turnbuckle 1¾"
Brake Beam   - Metal "Monarch"
Bolster   - Metal "Simplex"

Truck   - Arch Bar -Center to Center-Bearing 6'-7½"
Center to Center-Trucks - 28'-0"
Wheel Base of Trucks - 5'-4"
Axles   - 5"x9" Journals.
Wheels   - Eight 33"dia. 650"
Journal Boxes   - M.S.Cord Box & Cover.
Draft Gear   - Miners Tandem
Air Brakes   - New York.
GENERAL DIMENSIONS.
  Train Length   - 42'-11"
  Maximum Width - 9'-6"
  Maximum Height - 5'-2"
  Outside Length - 40'-0"
  Height Rail - Platform - 3'-10"

Total Number = ~~280~~
240

MODERN RAILROAD

The Alaska Railroad is now owned and operated by the State of Alaska. Formerly it was owned and operated by the Federal Railroad Administration, an agency within the U.S. Department of Transportation.

Today, the railroad operates 480.7 miles of single main-line track, extending from the deep-water ports of Seward and Whittier, through Anchorage, and on to Fairbanks. It maintains an additional 174.9 miles of branch line, sidings, spurs, and yard rails. These include branch lines running to Eielson Air Force Base, Fairbanks and Anchorage international airports, Palmer, and the Suntrana coalfields.

The Alaska Railroad forms an integral part of Alaska's economy. In addition to moving goods within the state, it provides a means of conveyance for the export of the state's vast natural resources. This export trade has taken on increasing importance in recent years, particularly in light of a coal deal that has been struck with South Korea. Also in recent years, the railroad's tourist business has increased greatly, especially the transport of passengers to the Denali National Park area.

Engine #1514 approaching the Tanana Railroad (now Mears Memorial) Bridge, 1974.

Lyman Woodman, Anchorage

Sign marking the site of the golden spike, near the north end of the Mears Memorial Bridge. Pictured are Col. and Mrs. Charles Debelius, U.S. Army Corps of Engineers, Aug. 22, 1974.

Lyman Woodman, Anchorage

On Aug. 22, 1974, the bridge over the Tanana River was dedicated the Mears Memorial Bridge. Pictured is Mrs. Robert Richards, granddaughter of Col. Frederick Mears, walking to the bridge with Walter S. Johnston, general manager of the Alaska Railroad. Lyman Woodman, Anchorage

The Mears Memorial Bridge has been serving the railroad since the structure's completion in the early 1920s.
Lyman Woodman, Anchorage

The railroad's last steam-engine run, a special excursion to the Matanuska Valley, took place in 1964.
Lyman Woodman, Anchorage

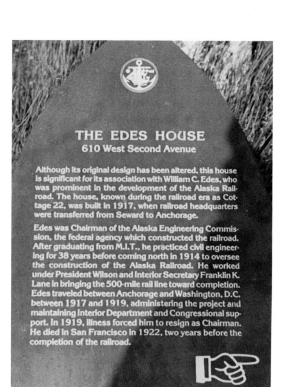

THE EDES HOUSE
610 West Second Avenue

Although its original design has been altered, this house is significant for its association with William C. Edes, who was prominent in the development of the Alaska Railroad. The house, known during the railroad era as Cottage 22, was built in 1917, when railroad headquarters were transferred from Seward to Anchorage.

Edes was Chairman of the Alaska Engineering Commission, the federal agency which constructed the railroad. After graduating from M.I.T., he practiced civil engineering for 38 years before coming north in 1914 to oversee the construction of the Alaska Railroad. He worked under President Wilson and Interior Secretary Franklin K. Lane in bringing the 500-mile rail line toward completion. Edes traveled between Anchorage and Washington, D.C. between 1917 and 1919, administering the project and maintaining Interior Department and Congressional support. In 1919, illness forced him to resign as Chairman. He died in San Francisco in 1922, two years before the completion of the railroad.

Marker placed here during Alaska Railroad Week, 1979.

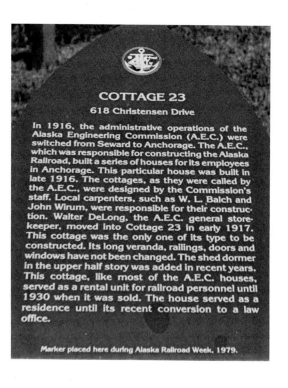

COTTAGE 23
618 Christensen Drive

In 1916, the administrative operations of the Alaska Engineering Commission (A.E.C.) were switched from Seward to Anchorage. The A.E.C., which was responsible for constructing the Alaska Railroad, built a series of houses for its employees in Anchorage. This particular house was built in late 1916. The cottages, as they were called by the A.E.C., were designed by the Commission's staff. Local carpenters, such as W. L. Balch and John Wirum, were responsible for their construction. Walter DeLong, the A.E.C. general storekeeper, moved into Cottage 23 in early 1917. This cottage was the only one of its type to be constructed. Its long veranda, railings, doors and windows have not been changed. The shed dormer in the upper half story was added in recent years. This cottage, like most of the A.E.C. houses, served as a rental unit for railroad personnel until 1930 when it was sold. The house served as a residence until its recent conversion to a law office.

Marker placed here during Alaska Railroad Week, 1979.

Former A.E.C. cottage on Government Hill.
Lyman Woodman
Anchorage

Engine 556, now on display at an Anchorage park. The engine was built by Baldwin for the U.S. Army in 1943. It was retired in 1956 and donated to the city.

The first locomotive brought to the Tanana Valley was a narrow-gauge 0-4-OST H.K. Porter #1792, built in 1899. Before it was purchased by Tanana Mines in 1905, it saw service in Vancouver, British Columbia, and Dawson, Yukon Territory. It was purchased by the A.E.C. in 1917 and retired in 1930. The engine, pictured here in the late 1930s, is now on display at Alaskaland in Fairbanks.

Author's Collection

The railroad's current station in Anchorage. A new administrative office building has been built behind this station. In right foreground is Alaska Railroad Engine #1, formerly used on the Panama Canal Railroad. Built in 1907 as a narrow-gauge engine, it was brought north in 1917 and converted to standard-gauge in 1930.

Remains of the old dock, built more than 50 years ago at the port of Anchorage.

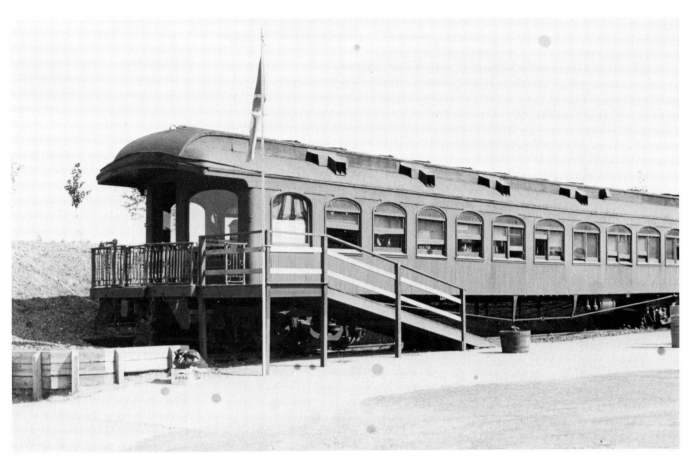

The Denali is now on display at Alaskaland in Fairbanks.

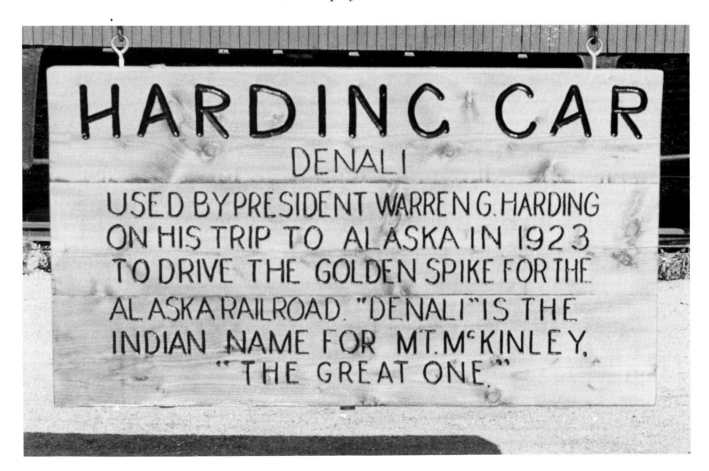

HARDING CAR

DENALI

USED BY PRESIDENT WARREN G. HARDING
ON HIS TRIP TO ALASKA IN 1923
TO DRIVE THE GOLDEN SPIKE FOR THE
ALASKA RAILROAD. "DENALI" IS THE
INDIAN NAME FOR MT. McKINLEY,
"THE GREAT ONE."

Bibliography

Clifford, Howard, *Rails North, The Railroads of Alaska and the Yukon,* Superior Publishing Co., Seattle, Wash., 1981.

Fitch, Edwin M. *The Alaska Railroad,* Frederick A. Praeger Publisher, New York, 1967.

Prince, Bernadine, *The Alaska Railroad, Vols. I and II,* Ken Wray Printing, Anchorage, Alaska, 1964.

Wilson, William H., *Railroad in the Clouds, The Alaska Railroad in the Age of Steam, 1914-1945,* Pruett Publishing Co., Boulder, Colo., 1977.

The author on Engine #1802 at Whittier.

ABOUT THE AUTHOR

STAN COHEN is a native of West Virginia and a graduate geologist of West Virginia University. He lives with his wife, Anne, in Missoula, Montana, where he is engaged full time in his publishing business. This is his second railroad book; the first was *The White Pass and Yukon Route.* Other books on Alaska he has written or published include: *Alaska Wilderness Rails; The Great Alaska Pipeline; Yukon River Steamboats; Queen City of the North—Dawson City, Yukon; Gold Rush Gateway—Skagway and Dyea, Alaska; The Forgotten War, Vols. I, II, III and IV; The Trail of '42; Flying Beats Work; The Streets Were Paved with Gold; 8.6—The Great Alaska Earthquake; The Alaska Flying Expedition; Highway on the Sea; Journey to the Koyukuk; Klondike Centennial Scrapbook; Soldiers of the Mist;* and *Make It Pay.* For a catalog of all titles write Pictorial Histories Publishing Company, 713 South Third Street West, Missoula, MT 59801.